Rock 'n Roll Recipes

Chef Rex Havick

with Illustrations by
Kelly Kennedy

This book was designed and produced by InfoPlus.

Kelly Kennedy, Illustrations
Paul Turner, Graphic Design
David Wiemers, Editor

Copyright © 1996 by David Wiemers and Paul Turner

Publisher's Cataloging in Publication
(Prepared by Quality Books, Inc.)

Havick, Rex.
  Rock 'n Roll Recipes/Rex Havick ; with illustrations by Kelly Kennedy.
  p. cm.
  Includes index.
  LCCN: 96-75246
  ISBN 0-9648684-1-5

  1. Cookery. 2. Rock music—Miscellanea. I. Kennedy, Kelly. II. Title.

TX714.H38 1996   641.5
                                        QBI96-20325

Printed in the United States of America
First Edition
1 2 3 4 5 6 7 8 9 10

InfoPlus
1012 Fair Oaks Avenue
Suite 124
South Pasadena, CA 91030

Dedicated to:
Rita Turner
a rock 'n roll mama
who was part of the British invasion of the '60s.

"The wine of Love is music,
And the feast of Love is song;
And when Love sits down to the banquet,
Love sits long."

- James Thompson, poet, 1882

"Shuttttt uppppp!!!!"

- Sid Vicious, The Sex Pistols, 1977

Table of Contents

Introduction

Even though Joan Jett and the Blackhearts take the credit, I swear I was the first to say, "*I love rock 'n roll*." There isn't a memory or event in my life that doesn't have a rock 'n roll song attached to it. "Aquarius/Let The Sunshine In" blared on the car radio the day I received my first driver's license. "In The Year 2525" had me rethinking the future as Neil Armstrong took man's first steps on the moon. "Fly Robin, Fly" and I were flying high the week I graduated from college. And "Like A Virgin" brings back fond memories that are, frankly, none of your business.

My career as a chef and tv personality has been a grand one. Still, friends wondered if I wrote this cookbook to release my frustrations as a rock star wannabe. That notion, I can assure them, is ridiculous. Okay, I confess, in high school I once formed a rock band. However, whenever we rehearsed, dogs barked, neighbors complained, and my electric guitar shorted out. I took this as an omen and quit. Instead, I traded my electric guitar for an electric blender and suddenly my creations turned my harsh music critics into admiring fans. My future was in a kitchen, not a recording studio. But whether creating haute cuisine in a fine restaurant, whipping up a dinner party for friends, or microwaving leftovers for myself, rock 'n roll music always blares in the background. So, like a computer, what goes in - must come out. After years of listening to rock music while I cooked, this recipe book spewed forth. Surely my friends and fans weren't expecting a gothic romance novel?!

This cookbook, "Rock 'n Roll Recipes," was inspired by the rock 'n roll songs that follow. They are recipes created or refined by me. They are not recipes from rock stars. Their job was to rock - mine to roll their songs into recipes. To each and every rock 'n roll artist represented here, my heartfelt thanks for their great music and culinary inspiration. Beyond that, to the many rock stars not represented here, again my thanks...and apologizes. Decisions and cuts had to be made, but hey, don't give up hope - that's what sequels are all about.

Enjoy these "Rock 'n Roll Recipes." I had a ball creating, testing, and sharing them with loved ones and fellow rock 'n roll fans. Put together a combination of these tasty dishes soon and have a rock 'n roll dinner party (see pages 182-183 for suggestions). With these fail-proof recipes, fine wine and good friends, you'll have a terrific time - especially if the background is filled with rock 'n roll music.

Now rattle those pots 'n pans, put on some music and shout "*I love rock 'n roll!*"

Chef Rex

Equipment

The television series "Lifestyles of the Rich and Famous" often features the homes of rock 'n roll stars. Their kitchens are fabulous. They have state-of-the-art-appliances, well-stocked cupboards, and a chef hanging around. If you're wondering, "Do I need all that to make rock 'n roll recipes?" - the answer is...some of it. I mean, if you have all that, why are you reading this book? Hand it to your chef, for crissakes!

Over the years, I've noticed that people who hate to cook often have tiny kitchens with plenty of cupboard space. On the other hand, people who love to cook never have enough cupboard space, no matter how large and spacious their kitchen. If you're reading this book, chances are you love to cook as much as you love rock 'n roll. Therefore, you already have most of the equipment listed - but nowhere to put it.

What's important to remember about kitchen equipment is this - whether purchased at a gourmet boutique or haggled for at a garage sale, the equipment is not nearly as important as your attitude. After all, it's possible to create classic dishes with only aluminum foil while camping in the woods - and just as possible to make unedible slop in a kitchen that Wolfgang Puck would die for. What's necessary for successful "Rock 'n Roll Recipes" is a willingness to experiment, a flare for creativity, and to have fun, fun, fun 'til Daddy takes your cookbook away.

With that spirit in mind, rock 'n roll cooks, don your aprons and make sure you have the following:

Stereo Equipment

A must for any serious rock 'n roll cook. Without inspiration how do you expect to create these recipes? A CD player is preferable, although tape decks, record players, radios and old phonograph players are acceptable, especially for vinyl die-hards. Apartment dwellers may want to be courteous and consider walkman headsets.

Pots and Pans

All shapes and sizes, and the heavier, the better. Personally, I try to avoid aluminum ware due to the possible link to, uh, what's that malady...I forget...oh, yeah, Alzheimer's Disease. Despite the expensive cookery I've acquired over the years, I still swear by good ol' cast iron. The secret to great success with cast iron is to season the pots and pans by never washing them in a dishwasher; instead, rinse them in hot water (using very little soap), scrub them clean, then heat the cast iron pot or pan on the stovetop to dry and kill any remaining bacteria. Do this faithfully after each and every use and your cast iron pans will last longer than the Rolling Stones' career.

Good Knives
There isn't a more pathetic sight than a dull knife attacking a thick-skinned tomato. It's how tomato soup was invented. Sharp knives are a must. Especially to throw at anyone who complains that your stereo is too loud (...just kidding...).

Food Processor
Whether Cuisinart or Sears, a food processor is the greatest invention since the sharp knife. It shreds, chops, dices and would be the perfect appliance if only it could clean itself. Also note: it will compete with your stereo for noise level.

Clay Roaster
If you don't already have one, rush...RUSH to the store and purchase a 3 or 4 quart clay roaster. If you're a cook who is all thumbs, this wonderful kitchen aid will instantly make you a chef to contend with. Soak the roaster in cold water for 30 minutes, put in your chicken, meatloaf and/or vegetables, stick it in a cold oven, turn the oven on to 450°F and wait for fabulous results. Chicken comes out moist and tender; meatloaf finally gains respect. Smaller versions for whole garlic cloves and onions are also a Chef Rex-ommendation.

Bundt Pan
Necessary for both cake and molded pasta recipes. Even mundane dishes suddenly have "style."

Pizza Pan
Not only essential for pizzas, but handy for recipes like "It's Too Late" Easy Potatoes.

Pasta Serving Bowl
Large, shallow serving bowls - great for serving pasta dishes. Sumo wrestlers also find them a convenient size for cereal bowls in the morning.

Stainless Steel Steamers
Needed to steam vegetables and tamales. Those with collapsible legs should be stored where they belong - *in the trash*!

Strainer
For draining pasta and vegetables...to straining soups - every kitchen should have one. Also adaptable as space helmets for kids come Halloween.

Barbeque Grill
A must for many "Rock 'n Roll Recipes." Nothing compares to roasted flavors fresh off the grill. Apartment dwellers may have to settle for small Hibachis, but they work fine, too.

Crockpot

Like the tortoise proved, slow and steady wins the race. A crockpot does wonders for stews, vegetable side-dishes, and hot ciders. Many "Rock 'n Roll Recipes," such as "Rock Around The Crock," are designed specifically for the slow cooker.

Microwave Oven

Convenient, but not necessary. There's nothing sadder than someone seeking instant gratification by standing in front of a microwave, shouting, "Hurry!" If you're one of these individuals - seek therapy.

Espresso Maker

A "yuppie" who doesn't have an espresso maker is in risk of having his/her "yuppie card" revoked. "Generation X" may want to forego the maker and just hang out at a coffee house. For everyone else, it's optional equipment, depending on kitchen size, economic status, and level of caffeine addiction.

Ice Cream Maker

Again, optional, but certainly fun. Those who make their own ice cream justify the extra calories they consume by the exercise they exert cranking the manual freezer. ...Yeah, right.

Mortar and Pestle

Great for crushing dried herbs, mashing garlic, and impressing friends with your culinary clutter. But really necessary?...well, no.

Graters

Grate, er, great for Parmesan cheese, whole nutmegs, and such.

Bleach Bottle

In a spray bottle, add 1 tablespoon liquid bleach to 1 quart of water. During cleanup, spray on countertops, cutting boards, and utensils to kill bacteria - especially after chopping chicken, beef, other meats, or raw eggs. With salmonella poisoning and other diseases on the rise - caution is wise. Prevention is easy, so keep the solution in a convenient place. Lemon-scented bleach even smells good, too. It's also a good idea to sanitize your dish cloths, wash rags, and pot scrubbers. Stick 'em in the dishwasher every cycle. If you don't have a dishwasher, wash these items regularly in hot soapy water.

Okay, rock 'n roll cooks, now that your kitchens are ready to rock, it's time to roll!

Recipes of the '50s

"Rock Around The Crock"

Bill Haley & His Comets

Bill Haley & His Comets blazed the trail to rock 'n roll. "Rock Around The Clock" wasn't the first rock 'n roll record, but it was the first to reach **number ❶** on the charts, where it lodged like a rock for 8 weeks. More importantly, it brought an awareness to rock 'n roll, a sound considered "underground" until Haley happened. To this day, "Rock Around The Clock" remains one of the ten most successful songs of all time. So is it any wonder music historians consider the song the root of the rock era and Bill Haley the "Father of Rock 'n Roll"? By the way, the term "rock 'n roll" is credited to disc jockey, Alan Freed, who spun the phrase from the 1947 record by Wild Bill Moore, "We're Gonna Rock, We're Gonna Roll." Way to go, Alan. And since "Rock Around The Clock" is considered the first rock classic, we honor it by making it the first offering in "Rock 'n Roll Recipes." This crockpot stew, like the song, is tasty, spicy, and thanks to the jalapeño chilies, will make things *"Shake, Rattle, and Roll"* (Bill's follow up single). Bill Haley passed away in 1981, but his records, his legend, and rock 'n roll live on. Hail Haley & His Comets!

The Top 10 Ingredients

1	tablespoon vegetable oil
2¼	pounds pork shoulder or boneless country-style spareribs, cut into 1-inch cubes
1	large onion, chopped
6	large garlic cloves, minced
1½	tablespoons chopped jalapeño chili
2	14½-ounce cans stewed tomatoes
1	tablespoon ground cumin
1	tablespoon dried oregano
1	15-ounce can kidney beans, rinsed and drained
1	15-ounce can pinto beans, rinsed and drained

Serves 6

Heat oil in large skillet over high heat. Season pork with salt and pepper. Add pork to skillet and sauté about 10 minutes. Add onion, garlic and jalapeño and cook another 5 minutes. In the meantime, listen to your old '45s from the '50s!

While you're listening to those old, pre-stereo jukebox favorites - transfer pork and onion mixture to crockpot. Add tomatoes with their liquid, kidney and pinto beans, cumin and oregano. Cover and simmer on low setting for 8 to 10 hours while you continue to listen to those golden oldies.

Mix beans into stew and simmer until heated through, about 10 minutes. Season with salt and pepper. Stop rocking around your crock long enough to enjoy dinner. Serve the stew with red wine and give a toast to the Father of Rock 'n Roll, Bill Haley!

"Hound Dogs" with "All Shook Up" Sauce

Elvis Presley

Elvis shook things up all right. He shook his hips, shook up teenagers, and shook up the music business by proving that rock 'n roll was here to stay. The King earned his imperial title by charting with more songs on the Hot 100 than any other recording artist in the rock era (149), a record even to this day. On top of that, he had 17 number ❶ hits and spent more weeks in that coveted position than even the Beatles. (Score: Elvis - 80 weeks/Beatles - 59 weeks) Even two decades after his early death, Elvis is still adored by millions of fans; in fact, his name is so recognizable worldwide, it's second only to Coca Cola. Ironically, his estate generates more income today than when he was alive - not to mention the income made by scores of Elvis impersonators. And to think it all started when record producer Sam Phillips found what he had long been looking for - "a white kid who could sing like a Negro." Elvis was truly an American phenomenon and, in his memory, we bring you these "Hound Dogs." Years from now these pups will still be American favorites, as will Elvis' pelvis shakin' music. Long live the King!

The Top 11 Ingredients

"All Shook Up" Sauce

- ¼ cup Dijon mustard
- 1 teaspoon dry mustard
- 1 teaspoon whole mustard seeds
- 1 teaspoon crushed black peppercorns
- 3 tablespoons brandy
- 3 tablespoons chopped fresh tarragon
- 2 tablespoons olive oil
- 1½ tablespoons white wine vinegar
- 2 teaspoons honey

"Hound Dogs"

- 8 jumbo beef franks
- 8 large hot dog buns

Serves 8

For "All Shook Up" Sauce

Create the right rock 'n roll atmosphere by playing old Elvis records in the background. Then, place all ingredients in plastic tupperware-type bowl; add lid, make sure it's secure. Next, do your best Elvis impersonation and shake it 'til it's "all shook up."

For "Hound Dogs"

Prepare barbecue and heat to medium-high. Brush "All Shook Up" sauce on those hound dogs, the beef franks. Place them on grill, turning and brushing them with more sauce occasionally. Grill dogs until slightly charred, about 7 minutes. Brush "All Shook Up" sauce on buns and place them on the grill, near the end. Remove once they start to toast, about 1- 2 minutes.

Place grilled hound dogs in buns - add more "All Shook Up" sauce. Serve...and remember to visit Graceland on your next trip to Memphis.

"Love Me Tender"loin

Elvis Presley

Elvis was as busy setting records as he was making records. "Hound Dog" was number ❶ for an unprecedented 11 weeks, a record that wasn't broken for nearly 4–count 'em–4 decades. Knocking that old "Hound Dog" down a notch to number two was Elvis' own "Love Me Tender," which set another record - it was the first time an artist had ever succeeded himself on the Hot 100. "Love Me Tender"loin will set a record with you, too - best tasting tenderloin in record time! This quick and easy dish for two features a creamy, tangy mushroom sauce. Guys, serve this romantic dish to your sweetheart and see if she doesn't swoon - just like girls used to do for the King!

The Top 9 Ingredients

- 2 thick beef tenderloin steaks
- 1 tablespoon olive oil
- 2 tablespoons butter
- 1 medium onion, chopped
- 1 teaspoon black peppercorns, crushed
- 3 ounces mushrooms, thinly sliced
- 2 tablespoons brandy
- ½ cup whipping cream
- 1 tablespoon Dijon mustard

Serves 2

Preheat oven to 375°F. Melt butter and olive oil in a large oven-proof skillet. Salt and pepper the tenderloins, place in skillet on the stove and brown each side 2 minutes. Place skillet in oven and cook an additional 5-7 minutes. Remove from oven and wrap steaks in aluminum foil to keep warm. Did you know the song "Love Me Tender" was taken from an 1861 folk song, "Aura Lee,"...but I digress...

Scrape and loosen the brown bits in the skillet and add onions, peppercorns, cooking until brown and flavorful. Add mushrooms and sauté 2 more minutes. Stir in whipping cream and Dijon mustard and stir until mixture boils - about 1 minute. Salt and pepper to taste. Spoon mushroom sauce over steaks and serve while watching an old rerun of Elvis' first movie, "Love Me Tender."

"Tutti Frutti" Cake

Little Richard

Little Richard - long career! At four decades, everyone is amazed at the longevity of The Rolling Stones, yet Little Richard had been rocking for a decade before the Stones ever started rolling. Richard Wayne Penniman (Little Richard) calls himself the "architect of rock 'n roll." Well, okay. Truth is, he's had more career comebacks than hit records, but hey, Richard Wayne, we love ya just the same. Hailing from Macon, Georgia, Little Richard's roots were in gospel and R&B, but black audiences rejected him. It wasn't until someone overheard his rock 'n roll song, "Tutti Frutti," and had him commit it to vinyl that record sales and fame followed. Later, he dropped out of the musical scene for a few years to serve as a minister, but came roaring back in '63, playing with several up-and-coming bands from England, namely the Beatles and the previously mentioned Rolling Stones. Over the years, drugs, family deaths, car accidents, and additional years in the ministry added more chapters to the Little Richard bio. But he's still around, still playing rock 'n roll, still an unfinished book. "Tutti Frutti" Cake, like Little Richard, is a classic, especially at holidays, and is destined to be a favorite of yours for the next five decades or so.

The Top 13 Ingredients

- 3 cups chopped pecans, toasted
- 2 cups chopped candied pineapple
- ¾ cup chopped candied cherries
- ⅓ cup chopped candied orange peel
- 1¾ cups plus 3 tablespoons all purpose flour
- 1 cup (2 sticks) butter
- 1 cup sugar
- 5 eggs
- 1 tablespoon vanilla extract
- 1 tablespoon lemon extract
- ½ teaspoon baking powder
  pinch of salt
  powdered sugar

Serves 12

Position rack in lowest third of oven and preheat to 250°F. Grease and flour 12 cup bundt pan. In large bowl, mix toasted pecans and fruits with 3 tablespoons flour. In another large bowl, cream butter with sugar until light and fluffy. Beat eggs with fork in separate bowl and then add to batter. Stir in vanilla and lemon extracts. Sift 1¾ cups flour with baking powder and salt. Add dry ingredients to batter; stir until blended. Mix fruit mixture into batter.

Pour batter into prepared pan. Bake until golden brown and tester inserted into center comes out clean, about 2½ hours. Cool in pan on rack 15 minutes. Turn out onto rack and cool. Dust with powdered sugar. Be sure and save a piece for *Long Tall Sally*.

"Gouda Golly Miss Molly" Potatoes

Little Richard

Good golly, Little Richard was hot in 1958. He climbed the charts with "Good Golly Miss Molly!" and in the process created one of the first rock 'n roll classics. Then Mitch Ryder and the Detroit Wheels re-recorded it in '66 and had even further success. So it seems fitting to bring Miss Molly back again, this time as a tasty 'tator treat. Thanks to the Gouda cheese, you'll say, "*Good golly*, it's good!"

Serves 6

The Top 7 Ingredients

1 tablespoon olive oil

1 large onion, chopped

1 cup whipping cream

1 cup half and half

1 teaspoon fennel seeds

2 pounds russet potatoes, peeled, thinly sliced

2 cups firmly packed shredded Gouda cheese (8 ounces)

Preheat oven to 400°F. Generously butter 8x8x2-inch baking dish. Heat 1 tablespoon olive oil in medium skillet over medium heat. Sauté onion until brown, about 7 minutes. Lower heat and add cream, half and half, and fennel seeds. Add potatoes to skillet. Bring mixture to boil, stirring frequently to separate vegetable slices. Boil 5 minutes. Season generously with salt and pepper. Transfer half of potato mixture to prepared baking dish. Sprinkle half of Gouda over. Top with remaining potato mixture. Firmly press mixture down. Sprinkle remaining Gouda over. Cover dish tightly with foil. Bake until potatoes are tender, about 40 minutes. Uncover and bake until top is golden brown, about 10 minutes longer. Let stand 10 minutes before serving which is plenty of time to check out Little Richard's performance in the 1986 film, "Down and Out in Beverly Hills."

"Blue Suede Shoes"tring Potatoes

Carl Perkins

The shoe industry, especially the makers of blue suede shoes, owe a nod of gratitude to Carl Perkins. "Blue Suede Shoes," both the shoes and the record, sold like crazy. The song was a high mark for Carl whose musical career evolved from country western, to rockabilly, to rock 'n roll. During the '50s, Perkins was one of the golden boys on Sun Label, along with Jerry Lee Lewis, Roy Orbison and that other rockin' kid...oh yeah, Elvis. Unfortunately, after Carl recorded "Blue Suede Shoes," he was in a near-fatal car crash. Unable to maintain his career, Carl saw Elvis' version of the song eclipse his own. Then drugs, depression, and drinking followed and Carl didn't pick up steam with his career until he toured with another buddy with similar problems, Johnny Cash. Both were able to put a happy ending on sad chapters of their lives. Carl's rock classic has now inspired "Blue Suede Shoes"tring Potatoes, bringing together a delicious yet odd combination of blue cheese and shoestring potatoes. Skeptical? Try it - it's so good you'll want to serve the controversial dish to guests at your next dinner party. They'll love the name - not to mention the dish. Just be careful not to drop any leftovers on your *blue suede shoes*!

The Top 9 Ingredients

1 20-ounce package frozen shoestring potatoes

2 ounces blue cheese, crumbled

4 tablespoons ($\frac{1}{2}$ stick) butter

$\frac{1}{4}$ cup olive oil

2 shallots, minced

2 garlic cloves, minced

1 tablespoon chopped fresh rosemary

vegetable oil for frying (preferably canola oil)

salt and pepper

Serves 4

Heat deep fryer to 375°F or place canola oil in large skillet 1-inch deep and heat to medium. Place frozen shoestring potatoes in hot oil and cook until golden brown. Remove and drain on paper towel.

Meanwhile, melt butter and olive oil in small saucepan on medium heat. Add minced shallots, garlic and rosemary and sauté for two minutes.

Place fried shoestring potatoes in bowl and toss in crumbled blue cheese. Pour hot butter mixture from saucepan over all and toss, mixing well. Salt and pepper to taste. Serve immediately. Surprisingly good, isn't it?

"Blueberry Chill"

Fats Domino

What's the skinny on Fats Domino? During the '50s, Antoine (as his mother called him) was cranking out hits as fast as he and his wife were cranking out kids (8 at last count...kids, that is - even more hit records). If you ask many of the rock 'n roll greats who influenced their music, time and time again you'll hear Fats' name mentioned. His marriage of R&B and rock 'n roll made him one of the decade's most popular entertainers. During the '60s, he was a favorite in Las Vegas at the Flamingo Hotel where he packed 'em in nightly. These days he's mostly retired in New Orleans. Since three of Fat's songs dwelled on a certain color ("Blueberry Hill," "My Blue Heaven," and "Blue Monday") it's only fitting that this recipe feature berries of that hue. And once you've tasted "Blueberry Chill" the only words to describe it are...*my blue heaven!*

The Top 8 Ingredients

- 4 cups fresh blueberries
- 1 cup water
- 3 tablespoons fresh lemon juice
- 2 tablespoons cornstarch
- 3 tablespoons sugar
- 1 teaspoon Amaretto liqueur
- 3 pints vanilla ice cream
- 2 cups fresh blueberries
  fresh mint sprigs

Serves 8

Combine first 4 ingredients in large saucepan. Stir over medium-high heat until mixture boils and thickens. Cool slightly. Purée mixture in processor or blender until smooth. Mix in sugar and Amaretto liqueur. Refrigerate until chilled, about 3 hours (I know, you want it right this minute, but *"Ain't That A Shame!"*).

Scoop ice cream into goblets. (For those of you watching your "Fats" intake, you may substitute "Fats"-free frozen vanilla yogurt or ice cream). Spoon sauce over. Top with fresh berries. Garnish with mint sprigs. You'll get *a thrill from Blueberry Chill!*

Chef Rex-ommendation!

You'll really get a thrill when you serve this with "Blame It On The Sugar" - Milli Vanilla Ice Cream (see page 152).

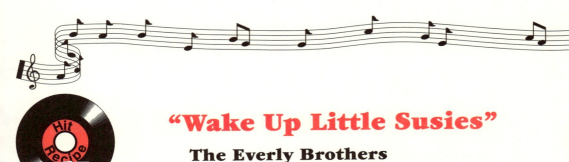

"Wake Up Little Susies"

The Everly Brothers

Scandalous! That's what people called the song, "Wake Up Little Susie," by Don and Phil, the wholesome and harmonious Everly Brothers. The song was about two teenagers who had fallen asleep at the drive-in movie - and in an era of "Father Knows Best" this caused frowns on many fathers' faces. Teenagers loved the song, though, and rebelled by sending it to number ❶. (Karma hit those teens, however; most are now fathers frowning over today's gangsta-rap lyrics!) In 1960 the brothers signed with a new label, Warner Brothers, for a million dollars. Many considered it an enormous sum for a risky venture; after all, many record executives weren't convinced rock 'n roll was here to stay. It was and the brothers tight harmonies influenced many rockers who followed, namely, the Beatles, the Beach Boys, The Mamas & The Papas, and especially Simon and Garfunkel. In 1973 they became the *Neverly* Brothers when Phil quit onstage during a performance at Knott's Berry Farm (the brothers reportedly didn't speak to one another for ten years). Many years later, Don Everly would have a famous rock 'n roll son-in-law (but more on that later). Now then, when you wake up tomorrow morning, treat yourself to "Wake Up Little Susies." It's a brunch-style egg dish with a combination of flavors that, like the Everly Brothers, blend together in perfect harmony. One taste and you'll say, *"Ooo, la la!"*

The Top 6 Ingredients

4 English muffins, toasted

8 slices Danish ham

4 marinated artichoke hearts, thinly sliced

8 poached eggs

   "That'll Be The Daise" - Buddy Holly-daise Sauce

   paprika

Serves 4

On each toasted English muffin half place 1 slice Danish ham, slice of artichoke heart, and poached egg. Top with "That'll Be The Daise" - Buddy Holly-daise Sauce (see next page). Garnish with paprika.

Chef Rex-ommendation!

Wake up! You don't have to use English muffins. Instead, try "Knead You Tonight" - INXS Bread (see page 149).

"That'll Be The Daise"
Buddy Holly-daise Sauce

The '72 rock classic "American Pie" refers to "...the day the music died." The date was February 3, 1959, to be exact, and it refers to the tragic day when young Buddy Holly's plane crashed. Only 22 at the time, Holly was killed but not before he and his fellow musicians, The Crickets, had given us songs like "Peggy Sue," "Oh Boy" and "Words of Love." Hollywood made a movie of Holly's short career and Gary Busey copped an Oscar nomination for his portrayal of Buddy. Today many rock stars credit Holly as an inspiration, among them Paul McCartney, who went so far as to purchase the publishing rights to Holly's songs. Buddy's biggest hit was "That'll Be The Day," which he claimed was inspired from a quote by John Wayne in the movie, "The Searchers." Now both the song and the quote have inspired this creamy, delicious variety of hollandaise sauce. Serve it today and if you don't hear *words of love*, you'll hear loved ones exclaim, *"Oh boy!"*

The Top 5 Ingredients

1 cup sour cream

4 egg yolks

2 tablespoons fresh lemon juice
pinch of paprika

2 tablespoons minced fresh herbs such as tarragon, basil or parsley (optional)

Makes about 2 cups

Beat sour cream, egg yolks, lemon juice and paprika in top of double boiler over simmering water until foamy and thickened. Remove from over water. Season with salt and pepper. Sprinkle herbs over sauce if desired. Good, isn't it, *Peggy Sue*?

Chef Rex-ommendation!

Buddy Holly-daise Sauce is also terrific on steamed vegetables, such as broccoli, cauliflower and asparagus.

Also good on freshly steamed crabmeat, topped with capers. So good - even the crab would approve!

"Chantilly Lace"

The Big Bopper

Talk about a tragic decision. The Big Bopper, a.k.a. J.P. Richardson, was a singer, songwriter, producer, and rockabilly performer who was also killed in the same plane crash that claimed the lives of Buddy Holly and Richie Valens. Sad thing is - the Big Bopper was not scheduled to be on the charted plane. He was going to the next gig via bus, but came down with stomach flu. Concerned that a long bus trip would prolong his suffering, the Big Bopper asked to trade places with one of Buddy Holly's new backup musicians which turned out to be a lucky break for the young backup named...Waylon Jennings! "Chantilly Lace" was The Big Bopper's big hit in '58. He also had a posthumous number ❶ hit with "Running Bear," which he wrote and produced for his protege, singer Johnny Preston. "Chantilly Lace" the shortcake dessert is dedicated to the memory of The Big Bopper and his bright musical career cut short...cake.

The Top 10 Ingredients

3   cups fresh strawberries, hulled
6   tablespoons Crème de Cassis
4   tablespoons sugar
1   cup chilled whipping cream
1   teaspoon vanilla extract

⅓   cup shortening
2   cups all-purpose flour
2   tablespoons sugar
3   teaspoons baking powder
1   teaspoon salt
¾   cup milk

2   1-pint baskets strawberries, hulled, sliced

Serves 8

Purée 3 cups strawberries with Cassis and 2 tablespoons sugar in processor. Strain to remove seeds. Cover and refrigerate until well chilled.

Using electric mixer, whip cream with remaining 2 tablespoons sugar and vanilla in large bowl to soft peaks.

Preheat oven to 450°F. Cut shortening into flour, 2 tablespoons sugar, baking powder and salt with pastry blender until mixture resembles fine crumbs. Stir in milk just until blended. Turn dough onto lightly floured surface. Gently smooth into a ball. Knead 20 to 25 times. Roll ½-inch thick. Cut with floured 3-inch cutter. Place dough rounds about 1 inch apart on ungreased cookie sheet. Bake 10 to 12 minutes or until golden. Split crosswise while hot and top pieces with sliced berries. Spoon strawberry sauce over. Top with whipped cream and serve.

Chicken "Lollipop"

The Chordettes

Can you name the group that had the distinctive honor of being the first musical group to appear on Dick Clark's "American Bandstand?" If you said The Chordettes, you're a winner. The female singing group from Sheboygan, Wisconsin, were winners, too - after they were discovered by Arthur Godfrey on his talent show. The girls had a sleepy-eyed hit in '55 with "Mr. Sandman" and "Lollipop" was a sweet success in '58. These sweet chicken lollipops will strike a good *chordette* with you, too, not to mention your friends and family.

The Top 4 Ingredients		
24	chicken drumettes	
1½	cups plum sauce (2 10-ounce jars)	
¼	cup soy sauce	
3	tablespoons cooking Sherry	

Serves 6-8

Preheat oven to 350°F. Holding drumette at base and using small sharp knife, push all meat toward top, forming "lollipop" shape. Repeat with remaining drumettes. Space drumettes evenly on baking sheet. Season with salt and pepper. Bake 30 minutes, basting drumettes once with pan juices.

Combine plum sauce, soy sauce and Sherry in medium saucepan and bring to boil over low-heat. Simmer for 5 minutes; cool. Remove chicken from oven. Spoon half of sauce over drumettes; chill remaining sauce. Bake drumettes until chicken is golden and crisp, about 15 minutes. Using tongs, transfer to serving platter. Serve with remaining chilled plum sauce. Are these suckers...er, lollipops, good - or what!?

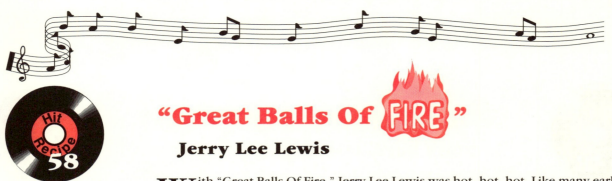

"Great Balls Of FIRE"

Jerry Lee Lewis

With "Great Balls Of Fire," Jerry Lee Lewis was hot, hot, hot. Like many early rock 'n rollers, Lewis' roots were in rockabilly. When Elvis left Sun Label for RCA, the record label was looking for a red hot replacement. Jerry Lee switched gears to rock 'n roll, replaced pelvis thrusts with outrageous antics at the piano - and got the contract. His fans loved his outrageous stage show and his popularity soared with hits like "Great Balls of Fire" and "Whole Lotta Shakin' Goin' On." The big shake down came however, when word got out that Lewis had married his 13 year old cousin. Concerts were cancelled and fans rejected him...in short, his red hot career was extinguished. Jerry Lee survived, though, and Hollywood made a movie of his life and named it after the song. Now there's "Great Balls Of Fire," the appetizers, and they're hot, hot, hot, too. Dip them in "Be-Bop-A-Lula" Sauce (see next page) and I guarantee there'll be *a whole lot of shakin' goin' on!*

Serves 4-6

The Top 11 Ingredients

12   whole red cherry peppers
4   ounces crabmeat, well drained
⅓   cup red onion, minced
¼   cup green bell pepper, minced
¼   cup mayonnaise
½   cup all purpose flour
½   teaspoon dried parsley flakes
½   teaspoon paprika
¼   teaspoon white pepper
¾   cup beer
    vegetable oil (for deep frying)

Starting just below stem, cut cherry peppers lengthwise in half, leaving stems attached. Remove seeds. Place peppers in medium saucepan. Cover with cold water and bring to simmer. Drain and let dry.

Combine crab, onion, bell pepper and mayonnaise in small bowl. Season with salt and pepper. Fill red cherry pepper cavities with crab mixture. Press pepper halves together to compress filling.

Place ½ cup flour in bowl. Add parsley flakes, paprika and white pepper; stir. Gradually whisk in beer. Let batter stand 30 minutes.

Heat oil in deep pot to medium heat or deep fryer to 375°F. Whisk batter until smooth. Holding stem end, dip each stuffed red cherry pepper into batter to coat completely and deep fry in batches until golden brown, about 3 minutes. Using slotted spoon, transfer "Great Balls of Fire" to paper towels and drain. Arrange chilies on platter. Dip them into "Be-Bop-A-Lula" sauce (see next page). *Goodness gracious, great balls of fire!*

"Be-Bop-A-Lula" Sauce

Gene Vincent

Capitol Records was looking for their "Elvis Presley" and held a talent search contest in the mid-'50s. Young Elvis-wannabe, Gene Vincent, wrote "Be-Bop-A-Lula" on the train going to the audition. Vincent not only won and recorded the song, which reached the Top 10 in '56, but even fooled Elvis' mother. When the King's mom heard the song, she congratulated her famous son, thinking it was Elvis singing. It was one hit Elvis couldn't take credit for. Gene's career, like many rock 'n rollers, was short lived and he died in 1971 from bleeding ulcers due to excessive drinking. His song remains a golden oldie, though, and this golden sauce is a tasty reminder of fun days, simpler times, and fooling Elvis' mother.

The Top 3 Ingredients
2   tablespoons Dijon mustard
2   teaspoons honey
½   teaspoon herbs de Provence

Makes ⅓ cup

Combine ingredients in small bowl; stir well. Serve with "Great Balls of Fire" and keep a fire extinguisher handy!

Chef Rex-ommendation!

Here's a golden oldie favorite of mine. Add 2 tablespoons melted butter to "Be-Bop-A-Lula" Sauce, stir well. Serve over steamed carrots. Garnish with freshly chopped thyme. Be-Bop-Carrot-Top!

Hit Recipe 58

"Johnnycakes B. Goode"

with Chuck Berry Syrup

This song may well be the first intergalactic hit. Chuck Berry's '58 classic, "Johnny B. Goode" is zooming through outer space at this very moment, part of the Voyager I, Earth's attempt to make contact with alien life. Aboard is a recorded message containing greetings in several foreign languages, and 90 minutes of music featuring Bach's Brandenburg Concerto No. 2 and Chuck's very own "Johnny B. Goode." Chuck proved to B. Goode at making hit records during the '50s with songs like "Maybellene," "Sweet Little Sixteen," and "Roll Over Beethoven." In '72, during a comeback phase, Berry scored his only number ❶ hit with his silliest song, "My Ding-a-Ling." These "Johnnycakes B. Goode" with Chuck Berry Syrup pay homage to the rock 'n roll legend. Any *Ding-a-Ling* can make these easy cornmeal treats, which are especially good when fresh berries are used in the syrup. Mmm, *Johnny, they B. Goode*!

Makes 2 dozen

The Top 12 Ingredients

Johnnycakes

 1 cup yellow cornmeal
 1 teaspoon salt
 2 tablespoons honey
 1 cup boiling water
 1 egg
 ½ cup milk
 2 tablespoons melted butter
 ½ cup all-purpose flour
 2 teaspoons baking powder

Chuck Berry Syrup

 1 pint fresh blueberries or raspberries, or cranberries
 1 cup water
 1 cup sugar

For Johnnycakes

In a medium bowl, combine cornmeal, salt and honey. Slowly stir in boiling water. Cover and let stand 10 minutes. In separate bowl, beat egg and add milk and melted butter; add to cornmeal mixture. Next, add sifted flour and baking powder. Stir batter until smooth. Pour batter onto hot, greased griddle or frying pan, turning once. Each cake should be approximately 4-inches in diameter. Serve with Chuck Berry Syrup.

For Chuck Berry Syrup

Combine all ingredients in small saucepan and cook over medium heat until syrup thickens slightly. Serve hot or allow to cool at room temperature and serve over Johnnycakes B. Goode.

"Lipstick On Your Cauliflower"

Connie Francis

What's the answer to Connie Francis' musical question, "Who's Sorry Now?" Undoubtedly, it's the many music labels that turned down Connie before MGM signed her up. In the late '50s and early '60s, Connie had a string of international hits like "Stupid Cupid," "Where The Boys Are," and three **number ❶** smashes, including "Everybody's Somebody's Fool." During those limelight years, the world had a love affair with Connie's upbeat, yet heartbreaking voice. Like many pop singers, Connie's career suffered in the mid-'60s during the British invasion. On top of that, personal crises occurred, i.e., a devastating rape and her brother's murder - and her career never fully recovered. "Lipstick On Your Collar" was a big hit in '59, though, and became a catch phrase for two-timing lovers everywhere. If you want to know *where the boys are* don't assume your boy is cheating on you with some dish. Instead, the dish he may be with is "Lipstick On Your Cauliflower." Even if cauliflower does has a B-O-R-I-N-G reputation, this creamy, yummy version brings new life to a dull vegetable. Be sure to make plenty, otherwise you could be the *stupid cupid* looking at the empty serving bowl, saying, *"Who's Sorry Now?"*

Serves 6

The Top 11 Ingredients

- 2 medium heads cauliflower, trimmed, cut into florets
- 3 tablespoons butter
- 3 tablespoons flour
- 1¾ cups milk
- 1 bay leaf
- ½ teaspoon ground nutmeg
- 2 tablespoons Dijon mustard
- 1 teaspoon Worcestershire sauce
- ½ cup fresh white breadcrumbs
- ¼ cup grated Parmesan cheese
- 1 teaspoon herbs de Provence
- 2 tablespoons butter, melted

Steam cauliflower florets in steamer pot with boiling water until crisp-tender, about 5 minutes. Drain. Rinse under cold water. Drain well.

Melt 3 tablespoons butter in small saucepan over low heat. Add flour and stir 5 minutes. Gradually whisk in milk. Add bay leaf and nutmeg and bring to simmer, stirring often. Cook until thick, stirring often, about 5 minutes. Stir in mustard and Worcestershire. Season sauce with salt and pepper. Discard bay leaf. Transfer sauce to large bowl. Add cauliflower to sauce and stir until well coated.

Preheat oven to 350°F. Place cauliflower mixture in baking dish. In small bowl combine breadcrumbs, Parmesan cheese, and herbs de Provence. Sprinkle breadcrumb mixture over cauliflower mixture. Drizzle with butter. Bake until cauliflower is heated through and sauce bubbles at edges, about 45 minutes. Cool 5 minutes and serve. Mmmmm...delicious! Get your collar ready - here come the kisses!

Recipes of the '60s

"Itsy Bitsy Teenie Weenie Yellow Polka Dot Zucchini" Dish

Brian Hyland

Novelty songs. In the late '50s and early '60s, songs such as "Purple People Eater," "Witch Doctor" and "Mr. Custer" were the rage, but none more successful than Brian Hyland's tribute to a teenie weenie bikini. Brian may have been a mere kid of sixteen when he took the song to **number ❶**, but he wasn't a one-hit-teenaged-wonder. He had several others, including "Sealed With A Kiss" and "Gypsy Woman." But it's "Itsy Bitsy...." that made more than a *teenie weenie* impression - and now we have this terrific side dish to remind us as well. The itsy bitsy teenie weenies are represented by the diced sausage; yellow polka dots are corn kernels; and granted, zucchinis are a poor substitute for bikinis - but hey, whatta you want from a recipe!? It's a tasty summertime dish that's *itsy bitsy* in the fat department to keep you looking good in that *teenie weenie bikini*.

The Top 10 Ingredients

2	cups diced zucchini (about 3 medium)
2	ears corn on the cob (or 1 10-ounce package of frozen corn kernels)
3	tablespoons butter
½	pound smoked Polska Kielbasa sausage
1	medium onion, chopped
⅓	cup diced marinated red bell pepper
2	green onions, chopped
1	jalapeño chili, seeded, chopped
1	large tomato, chopped
2	tablespoons chopped fresh cilantro

Serves 6

Dice zucchini and place in colander; sprinkle with salt. Allow to drain for 30 minutes; dab dry with paper towel.

Blanch fresh corn in par boiling water (not quite boiling) for 3 minutes, then remove kernels from cob. Set kernels aside.

Melt butter in large skillet over medium heat. Dice Kielbasa sausage and onion and sauté 5 minutes. Add corn kernels, red bell pepper, zucchini, green onion, jalapeño chili and sauté until tender, about 10 minutes. Add chopped tomato, stir until heated through. Add cilantro, salt and pepper to taste. Try to restrain yourself from nibbling *itsy bitsy teenie weenie* amounts before you serve it!

"The Twist" Pretzel Rolls

Chubby Checker

There's a twist to the success story of "The Twist." It started when Mrs. Dick Clark gave Ernest Evans the new name Chubby Checker, a "twist" on the name Fats Domino. In the summer of '60, Chubby gave dancing teenyboppers "twist" lessons on Mrs. Clark's husband's "American Bandstand." Several weeks later, the record rose to number **❶**. Chubby married Miss World '62 and later that same year, after an appearance on "The Ed Sullivan Show," adults were finally catching on to the twist craze. So the record company re-released the record. Not only did it go to number **❶** again (the only time an artist ever hit number **❶** twice with the same song), but it became the biggest record of 1962 - and the biggest selling record to this day! So the dance that inspired the song that inspired the recipe is now ready for you to try. For old times' sake, do the *twist* while you make "The Twist" Pretzel Rolls. Of course, what used to be a teenaged dance craze is now considered just good aerobic exercise.

The Top 11 Ingredients

2¾	cups bread flour
1	envelope quick-rising yeast
1	teaspoon salt
1	teaspoon sugar
1	teaspoon celery seeds
1	cup plus 2 tablespoons hot water
	cornmeal
8	cups water
¼	cup baking soda
2	tablespoons sugar
1	egg white, beaten to blend (glaze)
	coarse salt

Makes 8 pretzel rolls

Combine bread flour, 1 envelope yeast, 1 teaspoon salt, 1 teaspoon sugar and celery seeds in food processor and blend. With machine running, gradually pour hot water through feed tube, adding enough hot water to form smooth elastic dough. Process 1 minute to knead. Grease medium bowl. Add dough to bowl, turning to coat. Cover bowl with plastic wrap, then towel; let dough rise in warm draft-free area until doubled in volume, about 35 minutes.

Preheat oven to 375°F. Flour baking sheet. Punch dough down and knead on lightly floured surface until smooth. Divide into 8 pieces. Form each dough piece into long roll - about 8 inches long, then shape into a pretzel-like figure 8. Place pretzel rolls on prepared sheet. Cover with towel and let pretzel rolls rise until almost doubled in volume, about 20 minutes. Grease another baking sheet and sprinkle with cornmeal. Bring 8 cups water to boil in large saucepan. Add baking soda and 2 tablespoons sugar (water will foam up). Add 4 rolls and cook 30 seconds per side. Using slotted spoon, transfer rolls to prepared baking sheet. Repeat with remaining pretzel rolls. Brush pretzel rolls with egg white glaze. Sprinkle each generously with coarse salt. Bake rolls until brown, about 25 minutes. Transfer to racks and cool 10 minutes. Serve "The Twist" Pretzel Rolls warm or at room temperature.

"Mashed Potato Time"

with Dee Dee Sharp Cheddar Cheese

Sometimes it helps to have a "checkered" past. Just ask Dee Dee Sharp. Needing a job to help with household expenses, fourteen year old Dee Dee applied for a job at Cameo Parkway Records. The management, however, pushed her towards the exit door, until Chubby Checker walked in and said, "Hey, give the kid a break." They did and her song, "Mashed Potato Time" and the dance that inspired it became a mash...er, smash. Dee Dee had two left feet, though, and couldn't do the dance that made her so popular. Performing on "American Bandstand" she let the teenagers do the footwork while she sang. Dee Dee's follow up to "Mashed Potato Time" was "Gravy For My Mashed Potatoes" (was *food* on this girl's mind, *or what!?*). Two years later, she ran into Chubby again and this time they recorded a duet, "Slow Twistin'." This mashed potato dish will soon have you singing a different tune. You'll never want regular-old-boring mashed potatoes again. These cheddar spuds are so good, they'll make you wanna do the *mashed potato* dance!

The Top 7 Ingredients

- 2 whole garlic bulbs, roasted
- 1 teaspoon olive oil
- 2 pounds Russet potatoes, peeled and quartered
- 1 bay leaf
- ½ to 1 cup milk
- ⅓ cup grated sharp cheddar cheese
- ⅓ cup chopped chives

Serves 4

Preheat oven to 375°F. To roast garlic, soak clay garlic roaster in water for 15 minutes. Add 1 teaspoon olive oil to bottom of dish. Slice off the bottoms of the garlic bulbs, place bulbs in roaster with cut surface in olive oil, and bake for 20 minutes. Remove garlic bulbs from roaster and allow to cool. Separate the garlic cloves and squeeze out the soft garlic from the cut end of the clove into a bowl. The roasted garlic should have the consistency of butter.

Place potatoes and bay leaf in saucepan, cover with water and boil until tender, about 15 minutes. Drain. Discard bay leaf.

Place roasted garlic cloves in with potatoes and mash. Heat milk in microwave for 30 to 45 seconds until hot. Add milk and cheese to potato and garlic mixture and stir to desired consistency. Add chopped chives. Salt and pepper to taste. Delicious...and also great fun for food fights in dormitories and school cafeterias.

"Runaround Stew"

Dion

Talk about wanderlust! Singer Dion DiMucci was certainly on the go with hits like "Runaround Sue" followed by "The Wanderer" followed by "Lovers Who Wander." Before Dion was so busy wandering, he and the Belmonts (named after their neighborhood street in the Bronx) had a string of hits in the late '50s and early '60s. "For Bobbie" was one of those songs, written by a young man named Henry J. Deutschendorf (who would later change to a rocky mountain moniker, John Denver). "Runaround Stew" can be made in the morning, allowing you all afternoon to runaround. And it's so good, it'll keep your dinner companions from running around, for they'll want to stay seated for a second helping.

The Top 15 Ingredients

1	pound stew meat, cubed
¼	cup flour
1	tablespoon olive oil
2	teaspoons Bovril flavoring or Kitchen Bouquet
⅓	cup red wine
1½	cups beef broth
1	teaspoon Worcestershire sauce
4	carrots, sliced
3	potatoes, diced
2	onions, diced
1	stalk celery, sliced
4	parsnips, sliced
1	shallot, minced
1	clove garlic
1	bay leaf

Serves 4

Coat stew meat in flour, season with salt and pepper. Heat olive oil in skillet and brown stew meat on all sides, about 5 minutes. Add Bovril or Kitchen Bouquet; stir. Place meat in crockpot along with other ingredients except dumplings. Cover and cook on low setting for 10 to 12 hours. Stir before serving. It's especially good when served with Brenda Lee's "Dum Dum" Dumplings (see next page).

"Dum Dum" Dumplings

Brenda Lee

Brenda Lee didn't need to apologize for her **number ❶** hit, "I'm Sorry." After all, how many girls are sweet sixteen and at the peak of their career? During the early '60s, the little girl (4'9") with great big pipes had hit after hit with songs like "I Want To Be Wanted" and "Dum Dum." Eventually she got a two picture deal with Universal Studios, but movie stardom eluded her. Her records were produced by legendary Owen Bradley, the man responsible for many collaborations with Loretta Lynn and, most recently, k.d. lang. These "Dum Dum" Dumplings are aptly named because it's a no-brainer recipe that's a delicious companion to Dion's "Runaround Stew." But should you run out, you might sing, *"I'm Sorry."*

The Top 7 Ingredients	
3	tablespoons shortening
1½	cups all-purpose flour
2	teaspoons baking powder
½	teaspoon salt
¾	cup milk
⅓	cup shredded swiss cheese
½	teaspoon herbs de Provence

Serves 4

Cut shortening into flour, baking powder, and salt with pastry blender until mixture resembles fine crumbs. Stir in milk. Add swiss cheese and herbs de Provence; mix well. Drop dough by spoonfuls directly into stew. Cover and cook 20 minutes (1 hour if in a slow crockpot).

Chef Rex-ommendation!

Here's a suggestion that isn't too "dum dum." Serve these dumplings with "Nothing Compares 2 This Soup" (see page 159).

"Will You Still Love Me Tamale?"
The Shirelles

What made The Shirelles such hot tamales? Well, with "Will You Still Love Me Tomorrow," they were the first girl group in the rock 'n roll era to have a **number ❶** single. These four teenagers from Passaic, New Jersey, charted many times with such songs as "Dedicated To The One I Love" and their other **number ❶** hit, "Soldier Boy." But "W.Y.S.L.M.T." was their first biggie and their first collaboration with songwriters Carole King and Gerry Goffin. A decade later, Carole recorded the song herself on her "Tapestry" album, and many other singers followed suit - they know the song is a winner! And so is this tamale recipe. It's one you'll still love tomorrow...next week...next year! Tamales are surprisingly easy and fun to make. They also freeze well, so make plenty and store them in re-sealable plastic bags. And if you serve them with "Da Doo Ron Ron" Enchilada Sauce then *the one you're dedicated to will still love you tomorrow.*

The Top 15 Ingredients

Tamale Dough

3 large ears corn, shucked
2 tablespoons sugar
2 cups Masa Harina (corn tortilla mix)
½ cup corn oil
⅓ cup warm water
2 tablespoons chopped fresh basil
2 tablespoons chopped fresh mint
2 tablespoons chopped fresh cilantro
½ teaspoon baking powder
½ teaspoon salt

Cheese and Bell Pepper Filling

½ red bell pepper
½ yellow bell pepper
1 large green chili
4 ounces Ranchero cheese, crumbled

Assembly

Tamale husks (at least 10)

Serves 4

For Tamale Dough

Cut kernels from corn cobs and transfer kernels to large bowl. Blend 1 cup kernels and sugar in food processor until it's a chunky purée. Return purée to bowl with remaining corn. Add Masa Harina, oil, ⅓ cup water, herbs, baking powder and salt. Mix until soft moist dough forms, adding more water by tablespoons if dry. Set aside.

For Filling

Char bell peppers and green chili over gas flame or in broiler until skin is blackened. Transfer to paper bag and let stand 10 minutes to steam. Peel, seed and coarsely chop peppers and chili. Transfer pepper mixture to bowl. Mix in cheese. Season to taste with salt and pepper. Set aside.

Assembly

Cook husks in large pot of boiling water until soft, about 5 minutes. Drain. Flatten and overlap 2 husks on work surface, forming rectangle. Divide tamale dough into 8 equal pieces. Press 1 dough piece into 4-inch square in center of husks. Spoon $\frac{1}{8}$ of Ranchero cheese mixture onto center of dough. Place hands under husks and, using husks as aid, press tamale dough over to enclose filling. Next, fold 1 long side of husks over dough. Roll husks up, enclosing tamale dough completely. Twist ends of husks and tie with string or small strips of husk to secure. Repeat with remaining husks, dough and filling.

Place tamales in bamboo or metal steamer. Steam until cooked through, adding water to steaming pan if necessary as it evaporates, about 35 minutes. Transfer tamales to plates. Cut husks open. Top with dollops of sour cream. Serve to loved ones and accept compliments graciously.

Chef Rex-ommendation!

Your loved ones will still love you tomorrow if you serve these tamales topped with...

• "Da Doo Ron Ron" Enchilada Sauce (see page 36)

• "Hot Stuff" Salsa (see page 118)

• "Heartache Tonight" Sauce (see page 113)

"Spanish Harlem" Frittata

Ben E. King

Ben E. King drifted away from The Drifters when he ventured out on his own with "Spanish Harlem." The hit song was written by Jerry Leiber and Mike Stoller, the song writing duo that had more hits during the '50s & '60s than MacDonalds had hamburgers. They also wrote King's biggest hit, "Stand By Me," but by the late '60s, King's career was fading and he left his recording label. In the '80s, however, the movie, "Stand By Me," made what was old new again and King scored a nice comeback. "Spanish Harlem" was re-recorded by many artists, including The Mamas & The Papas and Aretha Franklin. Now it's a frittata favorite. Is it good? Sí...for yourself.

The Top 11 Ingredients

3   tablespoons olive oil

1   large russet potato, peeled, thinly sliced

1   medium onion, thinly sliced

1   small red bell pepper, seeded, sliced

1   small green bell pepper, seeded, sliced

⅓   cup green olives, minced

1   tablespoon chopped fresh thyme

6   large eggs

½   cup grated Parmesan cheese

2   tablespoons chopped fresh parsley

2   tablespoons drained capers

Serves 2

Heat 2 tablespoons olive oil in large skillet over medium heat. Layer half of potato, onion, red and green bell pepper slices, and green olives in skillet. Season with salt and pepper. Repeat layering and seasoning. Cover and cook until potatoes and vegetables are tender, stirring and turning frequently with spatula, about 20 minutes. Sprinkle thyme over. Cool slightly.

Whisk eggs in large bowl to blend. Season with salt and pepper. Add potato mixture to eggs. Wipe skillet clean. Heat 1 tablespoon olive oil in same skillet over medium-low heat. Pour egg mixture into skillet; sprinkle with cheese. Cover and cook until eggs are just set, about 10 minutes. Slide frittata onto platter. Sprinkle parsley and capers over. Cut into wedges and serve.

"Hit The Road, Flapjack"

Ray Charles

Is Ray Charles considered a musical genius? Most agree "un-huh." The ever popular singer has conquered the worlds of jazz, pop, blues, soul, country, rock 'n roll and even Pepsi commercials. Yet despite all the success, Ray's early life reads like a Dicken's tragedy. For example, at age four, he lost his brother to a drowning accident; at five, he lost his sight; ten, his father died; at fifteen, his mother passed away. But Ray overcame those tragic events and tasted sweet success. His first **number ❶** hit came in '60 with the now classic, "Georgia On My Mind," and his biggest hit ever was "I Can't Stop Lovin' You." "Hit The Road, Jack" hitchhiked to **number ❶** in '61, made Ray plenty of dough, and now has inspired this flapjack dough. The recipe has become a favorite, especially on holiday mornings. *I can't stop lovin'* this flapjack! Try it at your house today. And on the odd chance that someone doesn't like it, well, tell 'em to *hit the road, Jack!*.

The Top 10 Ingredients

3	large eggs
1	cup milk
1	cup all-purpose flour
½	teaspoon salt
5½	tablespoons butter
1	pound tart apples, peeled, thinly sliced
¼	cup sugar
1	teaspoon ground cinnamon
½	teaspoon ground nutmeg
	powdered sugar

Serves 2-4

Preheat oven to 450°F. In a small bowl, beat the eggs, milk, flour, and salt until smooth. Melt 1½ tablespoons of the butter in a large ovenproof skillet on medium heat. Pour in the batter and place the skillet in the hot oven. Bake at 450°F for 15 minutes, then lower the oven temperature to 350°F and continue baking for 10 minutes. The flapjack should be light brown and crisp. If it puffs up in large bubbles during the first 15 minutes, pierce it with a fork to deflate.

Meanwhile, in a sauté pan, melt the remaining 4 tablespoons butter and cook the apple slices along with the sugar and cinnamon, stirring often. Cook until apple slices are tender. When the flapjack is done, slide it onto a serving platter and pour the apples over the top. Cut into wedges, sprinkle with powdered sugar, and serve immediately. Then *hit the road, Jack!*

"Tossin' And Turnin'" Salad

Bobby Lewis

Good news/ bad news. First the good: Bobby Lewis was the first artist in the rock 'n roll era to have a debut record become the **number ❶** hit of the year. In the summer of '61, Lewis spent 7 weeks in the spotlight and secured the record's position as the best selling, most popular record of the year. In fact, "Tossin' And Turnin'" was the 4th biggest selling record of the decade. And for enquiring minds - those are the Swanettes singing backup. Now the bad news: after that success, Bobby slid into rock 'n roll oblivion. But, hey, better to have that moment in the spotlight than none at all. Like many double-sided hit records during the early '60s, "Tossin' And Turnin'" Salad is now a double-sided hit with "Sherry" Vinaigrette (see next page). Work them as a team and see if the spotlight isn't turned on you for creating this double winner.

The Top 7 Ingredients

2 heads Boston or butter lettuce, torn into bite-size pieces

1 head radicchio, torn into bite-size pieces

1 bunch watercress, stems removed

1 bunch arugula

2 celery stalks, chopped

⅔ cup grated Parmesan cheese

⅓ cup unsalted sunflower seeds

Serves 6

Combine all ingredients except cheese and sunflower seeds in large bowl. Add enough "Sherry" Vinaigrette with Four Seasonings to taste. *Toss and turn!* Sprinkle with Parmesan cheese and sunflower seeds then *toss and turn* some more. Divide among plates and serve.

"Sherry" Vinaigrette
with Four Seasonings

Think Mother Nature inspired the group's name The Four Seasons? Think again. Frankie Valli and his doo-wop buddies took the name from a bowling alley lounge where they once auditioned. The Four Seasons spent many seasons together before they finally had a **number ❶** hit with "Sherry." They followed it with four more, including the smash, "Big Girls Don't Cry." "Sherry" was written quickly (15 minutes) and rose quickly (**number ❶** in an easy 4 weeks, where it stayed for 5 weeks). "Sherry" vinaigrette is also quick and easy, and together with "Tossin' And Turnin'" Salad, it's a harmonious culinary duet. It's so good, there may not be any left for you. Should that happen, remember, *big girls don't cry*!

The Top 7 Ingredients

- ¼ cup Sherry wine vinegar
- 2 teaspoons Dijon mustard
- 1 shallot, minced
- 1 garlic clove, minced
- ½ teaspoon herbs de Provence
- ½ teaspoon dried parsley flakes
- ¾ cup olive oil

Serves 6

Whisk Sherry wine vinegar and Dijon mustard in small bowl. Add the 4 seasonings (shallots, garlic, herbs de Provence and parsley flakes). Gradually whisk in olive oil. Season with salt and pepper. Taste the Sherry? Mmmm...*ba-a-a-a-by!*

Chef Rex-ommendation!

Big girls don't cry if you substitute "Sherry" Vinaigrette for the dressing in "You Ain't Seen Nothin' Yet" Slaw (see page 101).

"Johnny Angel"food Cake

Shelley Fabares

The movie "American Graffiti" asked the question, "Where were you in '62?" If you were Shelley Fabares, you were **number ❶** on the music charts and America's **number ❶** sweetheart on the popular tv series, "The Donna Reed Show." Even though Shelley was once married to big-time record producer Lou Adler (The Mamas & The Papas) she always considered herself an actress, not a singer. Indeed, her career in television has been as sweet as she is (highlights: "The Donna Reed Show," "Brian's Song," "One Day At A Time" and "Coach"). But "Johnny Angel" was her big hit record, thanks to help she received from guitarist Glen Campbell, Hal Blaines on drums, and The Blossoms singing backup. The song reflected the teen innocence prevalent in America during the early '60s, an innocence long since lost. "Johnny Angel"food Cake is sweet innocence, too, and with it's red, white, and blue colors...very American.

The Top 12 Ingredients

Angelfood Cake

1¼	cup sifted cake flour
2	teaspoons vanilla
2	teaspoons fresh lemon juice
½	teaspoon almond extract
14	large egg whites
1½	teaspoons cream of tartar
1⅔	cups sugar

Johnny Sauce

2	baskets fresh strawberries, hulled
1	basket blueberries
⅓	cup sugar
1	tablespoon fresh lemon juice
¼	cup Amaretto liqueur
½	cup whipping cream
1	teaspoon vanilla

Serves 12

For Angelfood Cake

Position rack in center of oven and preheat to 300°F. Sift flour into medium bowl. Combine vanilla, lemon juice and almond extract in small bowl. Using electric mixer, beat whites in large bowl at medium speed until frothy. Add cream of tartar and beat until soft peaks form. Add sugar ⅓ cup at a time and continue to beat until whites are stiff. Fold in vanilla mixture. Sift flour into mixture, gently folding. Mix well, but do not overmix.

Spoon batter into ungreased 10-inch angelfood cake pan. Bake until top of cake is golden brown and springy to touch, about 1 hour 10 minutes. Invert cake pan over neck of narrow bottle and cool cake completely. Run knife around edge of pan to loosen cake. Turn out onto waxed paper-lined plate.

For Johnny Sauce

Place half of strawberries in medium bowl. Crush with fork or potato masher. Place half the blueberries in medium saucepan and crush. Add sugar and 1 tablespoon lemon juice. Stir over medium heat until sugar dissolves and juices become syrupy, about 4 minutes. Cool. Add to strawberry mixture. Stir in Amaretto. Let stand 20 minutes. In another bowl, slice strawberries and add remaining blueberries. Set aside; refrigerate.

Add vanilla to whipping cream and whip in chilled bowl until soft peaks form. Place in refrigerator until ready to use.

Assembly

Cut cake into 3 equal horizontal layers. In shallow tart dish, place one layer of angelfood cake. Place sliced strawberries and blueberries on top. Add next layer. Repeat with sliced strawberries and blueberries. Do the same with the top layer. Drizzle "Johnny" Sauce over entire cake. Garnish each slice of "Johnny Angel"food Cake with whipped cream. One bite and you'll hear a heavenly chorus singing!

"It's My Onion"
(And I'll Cry If I Want To)

Lesley Gore

Talk about being at the right place at the right time! Sixteen year old Lesley Gore was in a hotel lounge listening to a band, some friends of hers, when they invited her up on stage to sing. And who just happened to be in the same lounge that same evening listening, too? Try record producer Quincy Jones! He liked her/hated them. And the rest, as they say, is rock 'n roll history. "It's My Party" was both Lesley and Quincy's first **number ❶** record. Lesley had other chart hits, most notably "You Don't Own Me," which held at the number two position for 3 weeks. Keeping it out of the prized **number ❶** position was the first record by four lads from Liverpool who wanted to hold your hand. Don't cry for Lesley, though, she's done okay otherwise. Besides recording success, she received an Oscar nomination in '80 for co-writing the song, "Out Here On My Own," for the movie, "Fame." Now then, at your next party, you can cry if you want to, just be sure to serve this delicious onion appetizer. It's a party pleaser, especially when served with the Roy Orbison spicy tear-jerking dip, "Crying" Sauce (see next page).

Serves 4

Combine flour with Ranch dressing mix and other dry seasonings and place in large plastic bag. Mix well and set aside.

Peel onion but DO NOT slice off the root end. With a sharp knife, make 7 to 10 slices ¾ of the way down the onion making sure NOT to cut all the way through. Turn onion a half turn and make another 7 to 10 slices, so onion looks like a grid. Microwave on HIGH for approximately 1½ minutes. Remove and let cool. Press center of onion to open it, flower-like. Sprinkle with salt. Toss onion into plastic bag with dry ingredients. Shake until well mixed.

Heat oil in deep fryer to 375°F or heat in a medium saucepan to medium. Carefully drop onion in hot oil and cook until golden, 5-7 minutes. Remove with slotted spatula and drain on paper towel. Place on plate and serve hot or at room temperature. Pull "petals" off and dip in "Crying" Sauce (see next page).

The Top 7 Ingredients

½	cup flour
1	package Ranch dressing mix
1	teaspoon paprika
¼	teaspoon white pepper
1	large onion
	salt
	vegetable oil for frying

"Crying" Sauce

Roy Orbison

If Roy was "Crying," you can be sure it was all the way to the bank. Smash hits like "Crying," "Only The Lonely" and "Oh, Pretty Woman" made Roy an American music sensation during the early '60s. His popularity extended overseas, and in Britain he was so popular, the Beatles were *his* opening act. Tragic events fell upon Roy when his wife, pretty woman Claudette, was killed in a motorcycle accident; then his sons were killed when his house caught fire; and then Roy himself suffered a fatal heart attack in 1988...now make this delicious spicy sauce - before I start *crying!*

The Top 6 Ingredients

½ cup ketchup
½ teaspoon chili powder
½ teaspoon cayenne pepper
3 tablespoons honey
　dash of powdered cloves
　dash of lemon juice

Makes ½ cup

Place ingredients in glass bowl, stir and microwave on HIGH for 45 seconds. Let cool. Serve with "It's My Onion" appetizer, but keep kleenex tissues close by.

Chef Rex-ommendation!

You'll be crying tears of joy when you realize how many uses this sauce has. Try it with...

• "Great Balls Of Fire" (see page 14)

• fried zucchinis

• over cocktail shrimp

• mixed with cream cheese and served on sliced baguette

"Da Doo Ron Ron" Chicken Enchiladas

The Crystals

One thing is crystal clear about the Crystals - that wasn't them singing on their biggest hit record! The all girl group was under the guidance of legendary record producer Phil Spector, and the story goes like this... Seems Vikki Carr was about to record the song "He's a Rebel" on a rival label, but Spector wanted The Crystals to cut a version on his label first. Problem was, Phil was in New York and The Crystals were in Los Angeles. So Spector brought in backup singers, The Blossoms, substituted them for The Crystals, yet released the record under The Crystals' name. They beat Vikki Carr to the punch and it was The Crystals biggest hit ever. Little was thought of the substitution, yet 25 years later when Milli Vanilli pulled much the same stint, there was scorn, shame, and Indian-givers at the Grammys. Spector also produced The Crystals big hit in '63, "Da Doo Ron Ron," (and yes, that's really them singing). Singing backup on that song was an up-and-coming teenager named Cherilyn LaPierre, who would later shorten her name to Cher! Now we have "Da Doo Ron Ron" Chicken Enchiladas - the best enchiladas you're ever going to taste. They're a terrific casual weekday meal - or good enough to serve guests on your best *crystal* china.

The Top 11 Ingredients

"Da Doo Ron Ron" Enchilada Sauce

2	tablespoons olive oil
2	medium onions, chopped
5	garlic cloves, chopped
1½	teaspoons cumin seeds
½	teaspoons chili powder
1½	teaspoons dried oregano, crumbled
¼	teaspoon ground cinnamon
1½	cups canned enchilada sauce
2	cans tomato soup
1	tablespoon fresh lime juice
	cayenne pepper

Serves 6

For "Da Doo Ron Ron" Enchilada Sauce

Heat 2 tablespoons olive oil in a large skillet over high heat. Add chopped onions and garlic and sauté 5 minutes. Mix in spices and sauté 1 minute. Add enchilada sauce and tomato soup and simmer 2 minutes. Add fresh lime juice. Season to taste with salt and cayenne pepper. Allow to cool.

For Enchiladas

Prepare barbecue and heat to medium-high. Grill chicken breasts, 5 minutes each side. Remove, cut into bite-sized chunks.

Butter 13x9x2-inch glass baking dish. Mix 1¾ cups sour cream, chilies, ½ cup cilantro and cumin in large bowl. Mix in chicken, 1 cup grated cheddar cheese, chopped hard-boiled eggs, and chopped olives. Season filling to taste with salt and pepper.

Place enchilada sauce in flat shallow dish. Dip tortilla into cooled sauce, turn, making sure both sides of tortilla are coated with sauce. Place coated tortilla on plate. Spoon generous amount of filling down center of tortilla. Top filling with cream cheese strip, chopped green onions, and sprinkle with remaining grated cheddar cheese. Roll up tortilla, enclosing filling. Arrange enchilada seam side down in prepared dish. Repeat procedure with each tortilla until no more filling is available.

Preheat oven to 350°F. Pour remaining enchilada sauce over enchiladas. Cover and bake until sauce bubbles and enchiladas are heated through, about 45 minutes. Uncover, sprinkle with remaining 1 cup cheddar cheese and bake until cheese melts, about 5 minutes.

Top with remaining sour cream. Garnish with cilantro, if desired.

The Top 11 Ingredients

Enchiladas

- 4 boneless, skinless chicken breasts
- 1 16-ounce container sour cream
- 1 green chili, seeded, chopped
- ⅓ cup chopped fresh cilantro
- 1 teaspoon ground cumin
- 2 cups grated mild cheddar cheese
- 2 hard boiled eggs, chopped
- 1 4-ounce can chopped black olives
- 12 small flour tortillas
- 1 8-ounce package light cream cheese, cut into 12 strips
- 4 large green onions, chopped

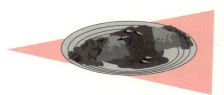

"I Wanna Mold Your Ham"

The Beatles

"The British are coming, the British are coming!" The Beatles hit the American shores, with other U.K. groups in the floodgates, and rock 'n roll was never the same. John, Paul, George and Ringo sold records and set records - many which may never be equalled again (see next page). For a nation still grieving the loss of its young President (Kennedy), the Fab Four were the first national distraction to come along. Their long hair, boyish good looks, and upbeat rock 'n roll made teenagers scream - and parents scratch their heads. Nevertheless, all America watched them perform on "The Ed Sullivan Show" (still one of the most watched episodes of television ever). Their single, "I Want To Hold Your Hand," zoomed to the top of the charts, held on for 7 weeks and became the biggest song of the year, not to mention the second biggest hit of The Beatles' career. In Britain it's still the biggest single to this day, with worldwide sales in excess of fifteen million units. This recipe, dedicated to the landmark song, may not create the kind of excitement known as Beatlemania, but it's certainly a tasty way to use leftover ham and fun to eat while you listen to "Meet The Beatles" or watch a video cassette of "A Hard Day's Night." Yeah, yeah, yeah!

The Top 10 Ingredients

- 6   cups dry bread
      (stuffing bread cubes can be used)
- 2½ cups cooked diced ham
- 2½ cups shredded Swiss cheese
- ½   cup chopped onion
- 4   eggs, beaten
- 2½ cups milk
- 1   teaspoon salt
- ½   teaspoon white pepper
- ½   teaspoon herbs de Provence
      butter

Serves 4

Butter the bottom and sides of a 12-cup bundt baking pan. Place 3 cups dry bread cubes evenly over bottom. Spread ham evenly over bread; then spread Swiss cheese over ham layer. Sprinkle with onions. Top with remaining 3 cups bread cubes. Beat eggs in separate bowl; add milk and seasonings; pour over mixture in bundt pan.

Preheat oven at 350°F. Place bundt pan in pan of hot water and bake for 1 hour. Remove from water pan and bake an additional ten minutes or until inserted toothpick comes out clean. Cool ten minutes before running spatula around the sides and inverting the pan onto a platter. Serve with buttered peas in center of ham mold (a veddy British tradition).

"If I Fell" Soufflé

The Beatles

Take a look at these records in the "Record" Record Book. In April of '64, The Beatles held the Top 5 records in the country, a feat that's never occurred before or since. And if those 5 weren't enough, there was a total of 14 Beatle records in the Top 100! At year's end, the Liverpool quartet had placed 10 records in the Top 100 for the year, which is still a record to this day, smashing Elvis' previous record of 9. A major newspaper called The Beatles the biggest news since World War II. America loved the Fab Four. "If I Fell" was a song from their first album, "Meet The Beatles," and was played on record players at top volume all around the country. Moms making souffles in the kitchen were having a tough time - after all, loud music, dancing and screaming Beatle fans don't exactly make a conductive environment for this delicate egg dish. And there's no guarantee your "If I Fell" soufflé won't fall either, especially if you put on a CD of the early Beatles and a nostalgic wave of Beatlemania comes over you. You may find yourself dancing and screaming just like the good old days. But fallen or puffy, this soufflé is a treat for the taste buds.

The Top 10 Ingredients

- 1   cup milk
- 1   tablespoon cornstarch
- ½   teaspoon dry mustard
- ½   teaspoon salt
- ½   teaspoons herbs de Provence
- 2   large egg yolks
- 1   cup packed shredded Gruyere cheese
-     pinch of cayenne pepper
- 3   egg whites
- ⅛   teaspoon cream of tartar

Serves 2-4

Preheat oven to 350°F. Lightly oil soufflé dish. Bring ¾ cup milk to boil in medium saucepan. Remove from heat. Stir remaining ¼ cup milk, cornstarch, mustard, salt and herbs de Provence in small bowl until combined. Whisk mixture into hot milk. Boil until thickened, whisking constantly, about 2 minutes. Remove from heat. Whisk in yolks, Gruyere cheese and cayenne.

Using electric mixer, beat egg whites, and cream of tartar in large bowl until stiff. Pour cheese mixture over whites and gently fold into cheese mixture. Carefully pour mixture into prepared soufflé dish. Set dish into deep pan. Add boiling water to pan - 2 inches up sides of dish. Bake soufflé until puffed and top is golden brown, about 1 hour. Serve immediately.

"I Get A Round" Steak

The Beach Boys

The Fourth of July...outdoor barbeques...the Beach Boys - all great American traditions. So how appropriate then that the All-American group that California girls loved reached **number ❶** with "I Get Around" on the Fourth of July, 1964. The boys saved our national face, too, by being the first American male group in over eight months to stave off the British music invasion by reaching the top of the charts. Even though the Beach Boys had charted with seven other records and were considered a huge success, "I Get Around" was their first **number ❶** and still remains the biggest selling record of their long chart career. In 1988, when the singing California surf dudes hit **number ❶** again with "Kokomo," more than 24 years had lapsed since "I Get Around," giving the Beach Boys the longest span of **number ❶** hits in the rock 'n roll era. "I Get A Round" Steak is guaranteed to be a hit at your next Fourth of July beach or backyard barbeque. This round steak recipe, like The Beach Boys, is All-American and summertime fun.

The Top 10 Ingredients

Steak

½	cup soy sauce
½	cup dry white wine
½	onion, chopped
3	tablespoons chopped fresh rosemary
2	tablespoons olive oil
2	garlic cloves, minced
1	2-pound round steak, trimmed

Sauce

½	cup sour cream
2	tablespoons prepared horseradish
¼	cup chopped chives

Serves 2-4

For Steak

Combine first 6 ingredients in glass baking dish. Add steak and turn to coat. Cover and marinate for 8 hours (or overnight), turning occasionally.

For Sauce

Put ingredients in small bowl, stir. Season with generous amount of pepper.

Prepare barbecue and heat to medium-high. Drain steak. Pour marinade into small saucepan and boil 2 minutes. Grill steak to desired doneness, basting occasionally with marinade, about 6 minutes per side for rare. Transfer steak to plate and cut to desired portions. Serve warm with horseradish sauce and have *fun, fun, fun* eating...*'til Daddy takes your T-Bone away.*

"Where Did Our Love Biscotti?"

The Supremes

The Supremes were supreme during the '60s. The trio had 12 **number ❶** records, more than any other American act during that decade and helped make Motown a top record label. "Where Did Our Love Go" was their first **number ❶** - but by no means their first attempt to get there. Originally named the Primettes, the three Detroit ladies were nicknamed 'The No Hit Supremes' by Motown onlookers since the trio's first eight releases went nowhere on the charts. But when Diana Ross, Mary Wilson and Florence Ballard teamed with songwriters Holland, Dozier and Holland, not only did they go straight to **number ❶** with "Where Did Our Love Go," but so did their next 4 releases - a feat no other American act had ever accomplished (however, it's a record Mariah Carey has since bested). On her own, Diana Ross has also had 6 **number ❶** singles, not to mention accolades in motion pictures, television...and soggy Central Park concerts. "Where Did Love Biscotti" is a supreme biscotti recipe. Its delicious blend of apricots, almonds, and white chocolate will have you cooing, just like Diana, *"...ooh, baby baby!"*

The Top 12 Ingredients

- 2¾ cups all purpose flour
- 1½ cups sugar
- ½ cup (1 stick) butter
- 1 teaspoon salt
- 2½ teaspoons baking powder
- 1 teaspoon ground ginger
- 3½ ounces white chocolate
- 1⅔ cups whole almonds, toasted
- 2 large eggs
- ⅓ cup apricot brandy
- 2 teaspoons almond extract
- 1 6-ounce package dried apricots, diced (dried turkish apricots, preferably)

Makes about 40 Biscotti

Line 18x12-inch cookie sheet with foil. Butter and flour foil. Combine first 6 ingredients in food processor, until coarse meal forms. Add white chocolate until finely chopped. Add toasted almonds and chop coarsely. Beat eggs, brandy, and extract to blend in large bowl. Add flour mixture and apricots and stir until moist dough forms. Drop dough by spoonfuls in 3 12-inch-long strips on prepared sheet, spacing evenly. Moisten fingertips and shape each dough strip into 2-inch-wide log. Refrigerate dough, 30 minutes.

Position rack in center of oven and preheat to 350°F. Bake logs 30 minutes. Cool. Reduce heat to 300°F. Cut logs crosswise into slices. Arrange on cookie sheet cut side down, bake 10 minutes, turn biscotti over, bake 10 minutes longer. Cool biscotti completely. Makes about 40. *Supreme,* yes?

"Hang On Sloopys"

The McCoys

During the '50s, record labels scrambled for the next Elvis; during the '60s, they searched for the next Beatles. Such was the case with record producer/songwriter Bert Burns, who was looking for four talented young guys with long hair to record his song, "My Girl Sloopy." Rick and the Raiders, a group playing proms, parties, and sock hops seemed to fit the bill. But another rock 'n roll group, Paul Revere and the Raiders, were causing a stir in the music scene, so Rick and the Raiders changed their name to The McCoys; Bert changed his song to "Hang On, Sloopy," and the rest is rock 'n roll history. The McCoys couldn't hang on to success, though; they eventually dissolved and became a backup band for rocker Johnny Winters. Paying homage to the song, we have "Hang On Sloopys," the sandwich. They'll be a hit with kids, so serve 'em at a birthday party, after a little league game, or...why not dinner tonight? They're tasty, fun, but be sure to *hang on to those sloopys!*

The Top 13 Ingredients

- 2 tablespoons olive oil
- 1 medium onion, sliced
- 1 green bell pepper, thinly sliced
- ½ cup sliced mushrooms
- 1½ pounds ground beef
- 1 small (4¼-ounce) can chopped ripe black olives
- 1 teaspoon fennel seeds
  Seasoning salt
  pepper
- 1 can tomato paste
- 1 cup water
- ¼ cup chopped fresh parsley
- 6 pita pockets

Serves 6-8

Place large skillet on stove over medium heat. Add 1 tablespoon olive oil, heat, then sauté sliced onion, green bell pepper and mushrooms until flavorful, about 5 minutes. Place in bowl and set aside.

Add 1 tablespoon olive oil to skillet, add ground beef and sauté until beef is well done, brown and crispy. Add chopped olives, fennel, seasoning salt and pepper. Stir until hot, another 2 minutes. Add onion, green bell pepper and mushroom mixture, tomato paste and water. Stir and bring to a boil. Reduce heat and simmer until thick, about 10 minutes. Add chopped parsley.

Warm pita pockets (if desired), and fill with "sloopy" mixture. Sprinkle with grated Parmesan cheese (optional, but highly recommended). Don't worry about leftovers - someone will pick your pita pocket! (Shew! Say that fast 3 times!?!)

"Brisket to Ride"

The Beatles

Ever see the movie "Eight Arms To Hold You"? Well, if you saw the Beatles' second movie, "Help!," then yes you did. Record collectors may note that on the 45 single, "Ticket To Ride," the label reads that the song was from the upcoming United Artists' release "Eight Arms To Hold You." Evidently, Lennon and McCartney never got around to writing that title song so the movie was retitled "Help!" to accommodate the song that they had written. Looking back on "Help!" and "A Hard Day's Night" it's easy to see the influence those movies had on music videos and the evolution of MTV. Now "Ticket To Ride" has evolved to "Brisket To Ride," a superb one-pot meal. It doesn't require much *help* nor will you spend *a hard day's night* in the kitchen preparing, but the meat and vegetables blend in perfect harmony, just like the great Beatle record from which it evolved.

The Top 15 Ingredients

- 3 tablespoons vegetable oil
- 3 medium onions, chopped
- 4 large garlic cloves, minced
- 2 tablespoons tomato paste
  paprika
- ½ teaspoon ground ginger
- 3½ cups beef broth
- 1½ cups dry red wine
- 3 bay leaves
- 2 teaspoons dried thyme
- 1 4½-pound boneless beef brisket
- 2 pounds red-skinned potatoes, each potato quartered
- 2 medium onions, peeled, quartered
- 4 large carrots, peeled, cut into ½-inch pieces
- 4 large parsnips, peeled, cut into ½-inch pieces
  fresh parsley, chopped

Serves 8

Preheat oven to 325°F. Heat vegetable oil in large saucepan over medium heat. Add chopped onions and minced garlic and cook until golden, stirring often, about 5 minutes. Add tomato paste, 1 tablespoon paprika and ginger; stir. Add beef broth, red wine, bay leaves and thyme. Boil 10 minutes to blend flavors. Transfer broth mixture to large roasting pan. Sprinkle brisket with paprika and rub in. Arrange brisket fat side up in roasting pan. Cover and bake 1 hour.

Arrange potatoes, onions, carrots and parsnips around brisket. Cover and bake until brisket is tender when pierced with fork, about 2½ hours longer. Cool 20 minutes. Transfer brisket to cutting board. Drain cooking liquid from pan into a medium saucepan and degrease. Purée cooking liquid in blender or processor. Return to saucepan and boil over high heat until reduced to 3½ cups, about 10 minutes. Season sauce to taste with salt and pepper. Thinly slice brisket across grain. Place on platter. Arrange vegetables around brisket. Spoon sauce over. Sprinkle with parsley and shout *"Help! I need someone"* (to help eat this) and watch 'em come running.

"Turn, Turn, Turn"
The Byrds on the Rotisserie

The Byrds made their nest egg with folk rock. When singer/songwriter Bob Dylan first combined folk music with rock 'n roll, he influenced many future rockers, including session players Jim McGuinn, Gene Clark and David Crosby. These three flocked together with Mike Clark and Chris Hillman to become the Byrds. They recorded Dylan's "Mr. Tambourine Man," which became their first record **number ❶** hit. In turn, "Turn, Turn, Turn," was their second **number ❶**, a song by another folk singer/songwriter, Pete Seeger. Doris Day's son, Terry Melcher, produced the Byrds' records and the band had a successful run for several years before they flew the coop, so to speak. Disgruntled with the band, David Crosby teamed up with friends Steven and Graham, disgruntled themselves with their bands, Buffalo Springfield and The Hollies, and together they formed...now what was that band called??? Anyway, "Turn, Turn, Turn" the Byrds is a yummy way to cook cornish game hens. A rotisserie isn't necessary, but helpful. If you *turn, turn, turn* those byrds by hand on the barbeque, the results will still be scrumptious. Oh yeah, and the name of that other band...Crosby, Stills & Nash.

Serves 6

Heat olive oil in small saucepan over low heat. Add shallots and sauté, about 3 minutes. Add apple jelly and chopped thyme and stir until jelly melts. Mix in vinegar. Set glaze aside.

Prepare barbecue and heat to medium-high. Rub "byrds" with olive oil and season with salt and pepper. Skew "byrds" on rotisserie blade. Brush glaze over each "byrd" while they *turn, turn, turn*. Reglaze frequently, until "byrds" are golden brown, approximately 45 minutes.

Arrange "byrds" on platter. Brush again with glaze. Garnish with apple slices and fresh thyme sprigs.

The Top 6 Ingredients

- ⅓ cup olive oil
- 2 shallots, minced
- 6 tablespoons apple jelly
- 3 teaspoons chopped fresh thyme
- ¼ cup cider vinegar

- 3 large cornish game hens or "byrds"

"Wild Things"

The Troggs

What happened to this generation!? That's what parents bemoaned when they heard "Wild Thing," a song that their Baby Boom teenagers loved. Despite those parental woes, the song went to number ❶. Now those Baby Boomers are parents themselves and are asking the even bigger question, "whatever happened to the Troggs?" Good question. Chip Taylor, who wrote "Wild Thing," recorded yet another version, a satirical one with Senator Bobby, a Robert Kennedy soundalike. That also made the Top 20, but has received little airplay in later years for obvious reasons of good judgement. These "wild things" are a delicious variation of potato latkes. Give some to your parents and see if, after all these years, they finally approve of "*wild things*."

The Top 12 Ingredients

1½	pounds red-skinned potatoes
1	9-ounce package frozen artichoke hearts, thawed, diced, patted dry
⅔	cup chopped leek (white and pale green parts only)
½	cup freshly grated Parmesan cheese
1	large egg, beaten to blend
2	tablespoons chopped fresh mint
2	teaspoons dried oregano
1	teaspoon salt
½	teaspoon pepper
6	ounces Montrachet cheese, crumbled
1½	cups (about) fresh French breadcrumbs
8	tablespoons (about) olive oil

Makes about 12 "Wild Things"

Cook potatoes in pot of boiling salted water until just tender, about 15 minutes. Drain. Cool completely and peel.

Preheat oven to 325°F. Place baking sheet in oven. Using hand grater, coarsely grate potatoes into large bowl. Add artichokes and leek. Mix Parmesan, egg, mint, oregano, salt and pepper in small bowl. Add to potato mixture. Stir in cheese and enough breadcrumbs to form mixture that holds together. Firmly press ½ cup mixture into 3½-inch round patties. Repeat with remaining mixture.

Heat 6 tablespoons oil in large skillet over medium heat. Place 4 pancakes into skillet. Cook until brown, about 6 minutes per side. Transfer to sheet in oven. Repeat with remaining pancakes, adding more oil to skillet by tablespoon-fulls as necessary. Serve hot. *Wild things, I think I love you!*

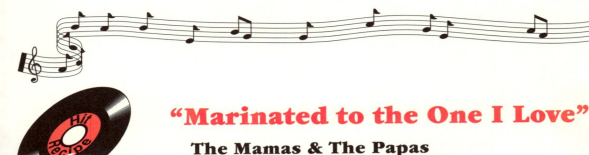

"Marinated to the One I Love"
The Mamas & The Papas

Men, women, large, small...John, Denny, Michelle, and Cass were all these things, including Mamas & Papas. In fact, John and Michelle's daughter, Chynna Phillips, later became ⅓ of the female trio Wilson Phillips in the early '90s. Brian Wilson of the Beach Boys provided the other ⅔, daughters Carnie and Wendy. The Mamas & The Papas were known for their lush harmonies and had many chart toppers, including a **number ❶** hit, "Monday, Monday." "Dedicated To The One I Love" was a remake of the old hit by The Shirelles and nearly made number one, stopping at number two. "Marinated..." is a superb chicken dish you'll want to remake many times, especially if you want to keep a *loved one dedicated to you.*

The Top 15 Ingredients

Chicken

- 3 tablespoons balsamic vinegar
- 2 tablespoons Dijon mustard
- 1 tablespoon chopped fresh parsley
- 1 tablespoon chopped fresh thyme or (1 teaspoon dried)
- 1½ tablespoons olive oil
- 4 boneless skinless chicken breasts

Sauce

- 1 tablespoon olive oil
- 2 green onion bunches, chopped (about 2½ cups)
- 1 shallot, minced
- 1 large garlic clove, minced
- 1 cup chopped fresh cilantro
- 1 green chili
- 1 cup chicken broth
- 4 teaspoons fresh lime juice
- fresh cilantro sprigs (optional)
- lime wedges (optional)

Serves 4

For Chicken

Mix balsamic vinegar, mustard, parsley and thyme in shallow bowl until well blended. Slowly whisk in olive oil.

Pound chicken breasts on both sides, making sure all meat is pierced. Add chicken to sauce and turn to coat. Marinate at least 20 minutes (the longer, the better).

For Sauce

Heat 1 tablespoon oil in medium skillet over medium-low heat. Add green onions, shallot and garlic and cook just until crisp-tender, about 4 minutes. Combine chopped cilantro and chili in food processor. Add onion mixture and chicken broth and purée until smooth. Return sauce to same skillet. Heat sauce over low heat. Stir in lime juice. Season with salt and pepper; keep warm.

Prepare barbecue and heat to medium-high. Place chicken on grill and cook about 3 minutes per side. Chicken should be cooked through, but still moist. Place each chicken breast on a plate and spoon sauce over. Garnish with cilantro sprigs and lime wedges, if desired, and serve.

"Monday, Monday"
Mama Casserole

Great voices often come in large packages. So it was with Mama Cass Elliott. When The Mamas & The Papas called it quits in 1968, each pursuing individual careers, Mama Cass had the earliest success, but also the earliest demise. In 1974 she died of a massive heart attack in the London flat of singer/songwriter Harry Nilsson (now deceased himself). When the corpse of Cass was found, she was naked in bed with a half-eaten sandwich by her side. Cass obviously loved food and hopefully she would have loved this "Monday, Monday" casserole, named in her honor. It's a quick and easy way to deal with leftover chicken and still have your loved ones think you slaved away in the kitchen. This "Monday, Monday" dish is just as delicious if served on Tuesday, Tuesday...Friday, Friday...or any day of the week, week.

The Top 13 Ingredients

1	package frozen egg noodles
3	tablespoons butter
¾	pound mushrooms, sliced
½	cup chopped onion
½	cup chopped celery
½	cup frozen peas, thawed
1	tablespoon Sherry
2	cups cooked chicken, chopped
2	tablespoons all purpose flour
1	can chicken broth
1	cup half and half
⅓	cup breadcrumbs
¼	cup grated Parmesan cheese

Serves 4

In large pot of boiling water, cook frozen egg noodles until tender, al dente, approximately 12 minutes. Drain; set aside.

Melt butter in Dutch oven over medium heat. Sauté vegetables until tender, about 5 minutes. Add Sherry and stir until it evaporates. Season chicken generously with salt and pepper, add to vegetables, cook another 3 minutes. Add flour to mixture, stir. Slowly mix in chicken broth ; stir. Boil until liquid thickens slightly, about 5 minutes. Add half and half and cooked noodles; stir. Simmer another 3 minutes.

Preheat oven to 350°F. Mix breadcrumbs and Parmesan cheese and add to top of dish. Bake until breadcrumb/cheese mixture is golden brown, about 35 minutes. Serve immediately. It's a dish your *Mama & Papa* will enjoy.

"Mellow Yellow" Jellow

Donovan

Have you never been mellow? Well, by 1966 the younger generation was mellowing out, tuning in, mindbending, letting their hair grow - and putting barbers out of work. It was called the 'psychedelic age' and during that period Donovan's hit song, "Mellow Yellow," had the older generation convinced that everyone under the age of 25 was smoking bananas. If you listen closely to the record, you'll hear the Beatles' Paul McCartney whispering repeatedly, "mellow yellow." Now's the time to search the attic, pull out your old hip huggers, Neru jacket, love beads, and put them on while you enjoy a terrific lunch of "Yellow Submarines" (see next page) and "Mellow Yellow" Jellow. Just make sure that banana ends up in your jello bowl and not your ashtray!

The Top 5 Ingredients

1	package (8 servings size) lemon gelatin
1	cup pineapple chunks
1	banana, sliced
1½	cups boiling water
½	cup vanilla ice cream, melted

Serves 8

In bowl, dissolve gelatin in boiling water; stir. Chill until thickened, approximately 2 hours. Add pineapple chunks, banana slices, and melted ice cream; stir thoroughly. Refrigerate until set again.

Chef Rex-ommendation!

Serve your fellow this "Mellow Yellow" Jellow in half a fresh cantaloupe. What a taste trip!

"Yellow Submarines"

The Beatles

The other "yellow" hit of '66 belonged to the Beatles. Everyone speculated whether "Yellow Submarine" was a musical journey through an altered state; and that theory became more widespread when an unorthodox animated film inspired by the song was released. The movie had a cool, warped Peter Max look to it which caused the establishment to scream, "drugs, drugs, drugs!" If you listen closely to "Yellow Submarine" you'll hear Donovan singing backup, returning the favor Paul McCartney did him on his 'yellow' song. "Yellow Submarine" easily influenced these submarine sandwiches. They're bodacious, cool...and very yellow.

The Top 9 Ingredients

1	tablespoon olive oil
1	large yellow bell pepper, thinly sliced
1	large yellow onion, sliced
⅓	cup mayonnaise
⅓	cup yellow mustard
½	teaspoon thyme
4	sandwich rolls
12	ounces assorted cold cuts
8	slices American cheese

Serves 4-8

Heat olive oil in large skillet on medium-high heat. Place yellow pepper slices and yellow onions in skillet and sauté until tender, about 5-7 minutes. Salt and pepper to taste.

In small bowl, combine mayonnaise, mustard and thyme; stir. Spread mixture on sandwich rolls. Next, add cold cuts, then top with American cheese slices. Top each sandwich with yellow peppers and onions. Cut each sandwich in half and serve. Now everybody sing, *"We all eat a yellow submarine...a yellow submarine...yellow submarine..."*

"Good Libations"

The Beach Boys

In retrospect, we have Beach Boy Brian Wilson to thank for the Beatles' musical maturation in the latter '60s. By '65, Brian Wilson was pushing his fellow Beach Boys beyond their surfin' music status into deeper musical waters, as evidenced in their **number ❶** hit single "Good Vibrations." The reflective moods and probing lyrics also contained in the Beach Boy album "Pet Sounds" prodded the Beatles to push themselves as well. The result was the landmark album "Sgt. Pepper's Lonely Hearts Club Band." So here's a toast to the "Good Vibrations" we were all picking up from Brian Wilson and The Beach Boys - and to the "good libations" their music continues to inspire.

"Little Juice Coupes"

3¾ cups lemon-lime soda

3 cups chilled cranberry-apple juice drink

1 cup chilled dry white wine

2 tablespoons brandy

Combine all ingredients in large bowl. Stir until well blended. Serve chilled.

"Fun, Fun, Fun" Hawaiian Smoothies

¼ pineapple, peeled, cored, chopped

1 cup vanilla ice cream

1 cup chilled pineapple juice
fresh pineapple wedges
fresh mint sprigs

Blend first 3 ingredients in blender until smooth. Pour into tall glasses. Garnish with pineapple wedges and mint sprigs.

"California Girls" Favorite

1¼ cups plain lowfat yogurt
1 pound ripe peaches, peeled, pitted, sliced
2 tablespoons fresh lemon juice
¼ cup honey
¼ teaspoon vanilla extract

Divide 1 cup yogurt among 8 sections of ice cube tray. Freeze until yogurt cubes are solid, at least 4 hours.

Purée peaches with lemon juice in blender. Add remaining ¼ cup yogurt, honey and vanilla. Process until mixture is well blended. Add frozen yogurt cubes and process until mixture is smooth and frothy. Pour into tall chilled glasses and serve.

"Slurpin' Safaris"

1 12-ounce can frozen citrus punch concentrate
1½ cups cold water
2 cups ice
2 ounces Absolut Citron
1 ounce Triple Sec liqueur

Place all ingredients (except Triple Sec) in blender. Blend until slush. Pour into glasses, float Triple Sec on top, and garnish with an orange slice and lime wheel.

"Kokomos"

1 cup chilled cranberry juice
1 cup chilled apple juice
1 small ripe banana, peeled, sliced
¼ cup sugar
2 tablespoons chilled whipping cream
1 tablespoon fresh lemon juice
6 ice cubes

Combine ingredients (except ice) in blender. Process until smooth. Add ice and process until frothy. Divide among 3 glasses. Serve immediately.

"I'm A Believer"

in The Monkees' Peanut Banana Biscuits

The Monkees had the biggest impact on the rock 'n roll scene since the Beatles - in a prepackaged-manufactured-sort-of-way. In the mid-'60s, NBC held auditions for a new tv sit-com with a concept that called for 'Beatlemania meets the Marx Brothers.' Mickey Dolenz, Mike Nesmith, Peter Torkelson, and Davy Jones beat out other warbling thespians who auditioned (including Steven Stills, Paul Williams, and several who eventually formed Three Dog Night). The tv show was a runaway success and the Monkee's song, "I'm A Believer," was the **number ❶** hit record of the year. It had a million order advance, the largest since the Beatles' "Can't Buy Me Love." The tune topped the charts for 7 weeks and was the biggest hit since the Fab Four's "I Wanna Hold Your Hand." Not bad for 4 guys who hadn't even learned to play their musical instruments yet. The song was written by a then struggling New York songwriter named Neil Diamond (whatever happened to him!?). The series petered out after two seasons, but the Monkees can still be seen on tv - at least in Pizza Hut commercials with ex-Beatle Ringo Starr. To help remember the tv show from the good ol' days, we have these Monkee biscuits. They're a lot like the old tv series: sweet, bananas, and slightly nutty.

The Top 10 Ingredients

3	cups all purpose flour
2½	tablespoons baking powder
½	teaspoon salt
¼	teaspoon ground nutmeg
6	tablespoons (¾ stick) unsalted butter
¼	cup plus ⅓ cup coarsely chopped dry-roasted peanuts
¾	cup plus 3 tablespoons (or more) whipping cream
¾	cup mashed ripe banana
2	tablespoons honey
⅓	cup crunchy granola

Serves 12

Preheat oven to 400°F. Combine first 4 ingredients in bowl. Add butter in small slices and mix until mixture resembles coarse meal. Add in ¼ cup peanuts, ¾ cup whipping cream and banana; stir until mixture begins to hold together. If mixture is too dry; add more cream, 1 teaspoon at a time. Gently knead dough on floured surface until smooth, about 2 minutes. Roll out ¾-inch thick. Cut into rounds using biscuit cutter or glass rim. Gather scraps; reroll to ¾-inch thickness. Cut out more biscuits. Place on large ungreased baking sheet.

Mix honey and 3 tablespoons whipping cream in bowl. Brush on biscuits. Sprinkle biscuits with ⅓ cup peanuts and ⅓ cup crunchy granola, mixed together. Bake until tester inserted into center comes out clean, about 20 minutes. Don't *monkee* around - serve 'em while they're warm!

"There's A Kind Of Hash"

Herman's Hermits

Herman's Hermits came out of seclusion long enough to rack up a few hit records. Two of the singles sung by the British teeny bopper heartthrob, Peter Noon (Herman), "Mrs. Brown You've Got A Lovely Daughter," and "I'm Henry VIIIth, I Am" went to **number ❶** in '65. At year's end the group had placed an impressive 5 singles on the Yearly Top 100. Like the Monkees, Herman's Hermits didn't actually play their own instruments in the recording studio - those honors went to session players (and future Led Zeppelin members) Jimmy Page and John Paul Jones. "There's A Kind Of Hush" was the Hermits' last single to reach the Top 10. Now we have "There's a Kind Of Hash" and after one taste, you'll be humming the lyrics to Herman's Hermits' first hit single, *"I'm Into Something Good."*

The Top 13 Ingredients

2½	pounds red potatoes
1	small red bell pepper, chopped
½	cup chopped parsley
1	small green bell pepper
2	cups diced cooked chicken
1	large onion, chopped
¼	cup fresh lime juice
1	jalapeño chili, seeded, minced
2	garlic cloves, minced
2	tablespoons canned chicken broth
2	tablespoons vegetable oil
¼	cup grated Parmesan cheese

Serves 4

Cook potatoes in large pot of boiling salted water until tender. Drain and cool completely. Peel and dice potatoes.

Mix ¼ cup red bell pepper and ¼ cup chopped parsley in small bowl and set aside. Mix remaining red bell pepper, green bell pepper, remaining parsley, potatoes, chicken, onion, lime juice, chili, garlic and broth in large bowl. Season to taste with salt and pepper.

Preheat broiler. Pour oil into large broiler-proof skillet. Add hash and press into skillet. Broil until top browns, about 5 minutes. Using spatula, turn browned portion over in sections. Broil until top is brown, about 5 minutes. Turn browned portion over again in sections. Press into solid round, add Parmesan cheese to top and cook until crusty and brown, about 5 minutes. Slide hash out of skillet and onto platter. Sprinkle with reserved red bell pepper and parsley. Cut into wedges and serve - saving a little for *Mrs. Brown and her lovely daughter.*

"Penne Lane"
The Beatles

And the winner was—? Two Beatle songs, "Penny Lane" and "Strawberry Fields Forever," were released as singles on the same day. Both were to be included on the Beatles' album, "Sgt. Pepper's Lonely Hearts Club Band," but as the album evolved they were dropped and issued as singles instead. "Penny Lane" emerged triumphant, peaking at **number ❶**, while "Strawberry" took forever to reach number eleven. "Penny Lane" was the Beatles 13th time in the lucky **number ❶** position (who said 13 had a hex!?). The song is Paul McCartney's nostalgic look at life in Liverpool and "Penne Lane," the pasta dish, is a nostalgic favorite of mine. The fresher the ingredients, the better the results. Use them and it's guaranteed the dish will become a favorite of yours, too. It's nostalgia in the making.

The Top 10 Ingredients

¼ cup olive oil

3 large garlic cloves, minced

½ pound mushrooms, sliced

4 tomatoes, chopped

2 tablespoons chopped fresh oregano

½ cup frozen baby peas, thawed

½ cup crumbled gorgonzola cheese

1 pound penne

⅓ cup toasted pine nuts

2 tablespoons chopped fresh basil

Serves 4

Heat olive oil in large skillet over medium-high heat. Add garlic; sauté 1 minute. Add mushrooms; sauté until soft, about 5 minutes. Add tomatoes, oregano and simmer until sauce thickens slightly, about 5 minutes. Place frozen peas in strainer and hold under hot tap water until thawed. Add to sauce along with gorgonzola; stir until cheese is melted, about 1 minute. Remove from heat.

Meanwhile, cook penne in large pot of boiling salted water (plus one teaspoon olive oil) until al dente (tender but still firm to bite). Drain. Add pasta to sauce in skillet and toss until well-mixed. Season to taste with salt and pepper. Transfer pasta to bowl. Sprinkle with toasted pine nuts and chopped basil and serve. Be sure to save enough room for "Strawberry Pie Forever" (see next page).

"Strawberry Pie Forever"
The Beatles

Paul is dead. Remember that rumor? Back in the late '60s, the storymill was working overtime speculating that Beatle Paul McCartney had expired and a look-a-like had filled his shoes. Fueling that speculation were "clues," such as the one at the end of the song, "Strawberry Fields Forever" - John Lennon is heard moaning (supposedly) "I buried Paul." Actually, he's saying, "Cranberry Sauce." While listening to the old record again, if you're still convinced John is speaking of Paul's internment, yet you have this uncontrollable (subliminal) urge for cranberry sauce, I urge you to make "Linger," the cranberries (sauce),(see page 176). In the meantime, enjoy this scrumptious pie. After tasting the Pecan Allspice Crust, you'll find regular crusts to be...well, flaky. Use fresh berries in season and you'll want to eat this *strawberry pie...forever!*

Serves 6

The Top 13 Ingredients

Pecan Allspice Crust

- ¾ cup all purpose flour
- 6 tablespoons firmly packed golden brown sugar
- ¼ teaspoon salt
- ½ teaspoon ground allspice
- 6 tablespoons (¾ stick) unsalted butter, cut into pieces
- 1 tablespoon cold water
- ½ cup finely chopped toasted pecans

Strawberry Filling Forever

- 3 baskets fresh strawberries
- 1 cup sugar
- 3 tablespoons cornstarch
- ½ cup water
  few drops red food color, if desired
- ¼ cup chopped fresh mint leaves

For Crust

Position rack in center of oven and preheat to 375°F. Butter 9-inch pie tin. Blend flour, sugar, salt and allspice in food processor using pulse. Add butter and process until mixture resembles coarse meal. Add water and process just until moist clumps form. Transfer to large bowl. Add finely chopped toasted pecans and knead gently until pecans are incorporated and dough comes together. Refrigerate until dough is firm, about 30 minutes. On floured board, roll out dough and press on bottom and up sides of prepared pan. Line crust with foil; fill with dry beans or pie weights. Bake until crust sides are firm, about 10 minutes. Transfer crust to rack. Let cool.

For Filling

Mash enough strawberries to measure 1 cup. Mix sugar and cornstarch in saucepan. Gradually stir in water, food color and mashed strawberries. Cook over medium heat, stirring constantly, until moisture thickens and boils for 1 minute; cool. Clean and hull the remainder of the strawberries. Place in pie shell. Pour cooked and cooled strawberry mixture over top. Sprinkle mint leaves on top. Refrigerate several hours before serving. Top with whipped cream, if desired.

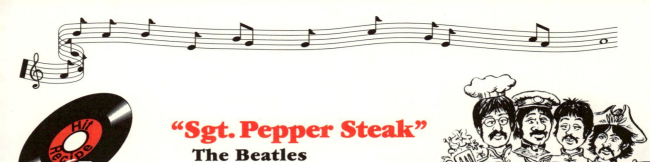

"Sgt. Pepper Steak"
The Beatles

The Beatles' concept album, "Sgt. Pepper's Lonely Heart's Club Band" is considered by many rock critics to be the most important album of the 20th century. By the late '60s, the Beatles had changed their look, experimented with new sounds (like sitars), and had everyone speculating as to what that album cover represented. It was decided early on that none of the songs from the album were to be issued as singles. Nevertheless, many songs found their way to the airwaves over the past few decades, including the two represented here, "When I'm Sixty-Four" and the title track, "Sgt. Pepper's Lonely Heart Club Band." The scrumptious "Sgt. Pepper Steak" could be considered a 'concept' steak. The many pepper flavors should not be considered by the faint of heart...or lonely hearts, for that matter. If you can't eat an entire serving - don't worry, *you'll get by with a little help from your friends.*

Serves 6

For Sauce

Whisk all ingredients in small bowl. Cover and refrigerate until ready to serve.

For Steaks

Coarsely grind all peppercorns in spice grinder or blender. Transfer peppercorns to bowl. Mix in salt. Whisk mustard, butter and 1 cup chopped parsley in medium bowl to blend. Rub all over tenderloins. Roll each tenderloin in peppercorn mixture, coating completely.

Preheat oven to 450°F. Place tenderloins on rack set in shallow baking pan. Turning once or twice, roast until meat thermometer inserted into center registers 130°F for rare, about 3-5 minutes. Transfer steaks to platter. Let stand a few minutes. Cut steaks into slices, arrange on platter, and surround with parsley. Serve with sauce. Mmm...good album...good steak.

The Top 13 Ingredients

Sauce

- 1 cup sour cream
- 3 tablespoons Dijon mustard
- 2 tablespoons prepared horseradish
- 1 teaspoon fresh lemon juice

Steaks

- 2 teaspoons whole black peppercorns
- 2 teaspoons whole white peppercorns
- 2 teaspoons whole green peppercorns
- 2 teaspoons coarse salt
- 3 tablespoons Dijon mustard
- 2 tablespoons (¼ stick) butter, room temperature
- 1 cup loosely packed fresh parsley, chopped
- 2 1-pound beef tenderloin steaks, trimmed
-     additional fresh parsley

"When I'm Sixty-Four" Prune Muffins

The Beatles

The Fab Four were still in their 20s when they sang this song about the "golden years." These days the remaining Fab Three are closer to 64 than they'll ever be to 20 again. Tasting these delicious muffins, you'll wonder if the Beatles were actually singing, "will you still *knead* me, will you still feed me..." Well, no need to knead this dough, just make sure it's well-stirred. And be careful not to overbake the muffins (again, think "golden"), otherwise they dry out quickly. Don't get the notion that these prune muffins are only for old folks, either. You'll also get appreciative smiles when you serve them to young whippersnappers - like the grandchildren from the song, *Vera, Chuck, and Dave.*

The Top 16 Ingredients

Topping

 2 tablespoons brown sugar

 2 tablespoons chopped walnuts

 ¼ teaspoon ground cinnamon

Batter

 2 cups all purpose flour

 1¼ cups sugar

 2 teaspoons baking powder

 1 teaspoon baking soda

 ¼ teaspoon salt

 1 cup chopped dried pitted prunes

 ½ cup chopped walnuts

 1 large egg

 1 large egg yolk

 1 cup sour cream

 6 tablespoons (¾ stick) butter

 2 tablespoons milk

 1 teaspoon vanilla extract

Serves 12

For Topping

Mix all ingredients together in small bowl. Set aside.

For Batter

Preheat oven to 400°F. Butter twelve ½ cup muffin cups or line with paper liners. Sift first 5 ingredients into large bowl. Add prunes and walnuts; stir to combine. Whisk egg and yolk together in medium bowl. Add sour cream, butter, milk and vanilla. Stir until smooth. Make a well in the center of the flour mixture. Add egg mixture and stir until just combined. Divide batter among prepared cups. Sprinkle each with topping. Bake until tester inserted into centers comes out clean, about 25 minutes. Invert muffins onto rack and cool slightly before serving.

Chef Rex-ommendation!

⅓ cup cholesterol-free egg beaters may be substituted for egg and egg yolk. After all, at 64 (or approaching) we need to watch what we eat!

"Ode To Sloppie Joe"

Bobbie Gentry

Where did this song come from!? In an era dominated by male rock groups, pretty lady Bobbie Gentry did the unexpected. Her moody and mysterious ballad, "Ode To Billie Joe," caught radio listeners pleasantly off-guard and snuck onto the music charts. No sooner had Billie Joe jumped down off the Tallahatchee bridge, than the record jumped up the charts and landed at **number ❶** for four weeks. The

song also landed at number four at year's end and won a shelf of Grammys for Gentry, a southern belle who took her name from a Charleton Heston film, "Ruby Gentry." This good ol' southern recipe is an ode to Bobbie Gentry, an ode to Billie Joe, and most importantly, an ode to sloppy joes. Go ahead, jump into one!

Serves 6

The Top 13 Ingredients

1	tablespoon olive oil
1½	pounds ground beef
2	medium onions, chopped
1	green bell pepper, chopped
4	large garlic cloves, minced
1½	tablespoons chili powder
2	28-ounce cans plum tomatoes, drained, chopped
½	cup chili sauce
½	cup canned beef broth
2	teaspoons red wine vinegar
2	teaspoons Worcestershire sauce
¼	cup chopped fresh parsley
6	hamburger buns or onion rolls

Heat olive oil in large skillet over high heat. Add beef and cook until brown and flavorful, stirring often. Mix in onions, green bell pepper and garlic. Cook another 5 minutes. Mix in chili powder and stir 1 minute. Add tomatoes, chili sauce, beef broth, vinegar and Worcestershire sauce. Cook until vegetables are tender and mixture is thick, stirring occasionally, about 20 minutes. Season to taste with salt and pepper. Mix in parsley and serve on grilled hamburger buns or onion rolls, open faced. Eat while watching the movie version of "Ode To Billie Joe," starring Robby Benson and directed by Max (Jethro Clampett of "The Beverly Hillbillies") Baer.

Chef Rex-ommendation!

Substitute "Careless Whimpers" Spicy Ketchup for chili sauce (see page 142).

"Respect" Rouille

on Queen of Sole - Aretha Franklin

What comedian Rodney Dangerfield yearns for is what Aretha Franklin sings about and gets. "Respect" was Aretha's first song to top the charts at **number ❶** and she's been getting R-E-S-P-E-C-T ever since. With six consecutive Top 10 hits following "Respect," Aretha earned the title "Lady Soul." And since she continues to make records year after year, decade after decade, earning new fans with new generations, Miss Franklin's royal reputation has earned her the more accurate title, "Queen of Soul." Crank up the Queen's records loud as you prepare this soulful sole food. And remember, this rouille, like Aretha, should be served with the *"respect"* it deserves.

The Top 9 Ingredients

½   cup olive oil

⅓   cup white wine vinegar

1   shallot, minced

2   tablespoons garlic, minced

4   teaspoons fresh lemon juice

4   4-ounce sole fillets

1   cup whipping cream

1   teaspoon dry white wine

½   cup chopped fresh parsley

Serves 4

Mix oil, vinegar, half of minced shallots, 1 tablespoon garlic and 2 teaspoons lemon juice in small baking dish. Add fish and turn to coat. Cover and refrigerate 1 hour.

Boil cream, wine, remaining 1 tablespoon garlic, remaining shallots, and 2 teaspoons lemon juice in small saucepan over medium heat until reduced to ½ cup, about 5 minutes. Set aside.

Remove fish from marinade. Heat large skillet over medium-high heat. Add fish and sauté just until cooked through, about 2 minutes per side. Transfer to plates. Bring sauce to simmer. Mix in parsley. Spoon over fish. Be sure and listen to an Aretha CD while eating. When she sings - she's really cooking!

"Light My FIRE" Salad
The Doors

Many doors opened for the Doors during the summer of '67. The door to success was opened by their single, "Light My Fire." It sizzled and went straight to number **❶**, was the second biggest hit of the year, and an instant rock classic. The door to opportunity continued as the group charted many more times during the next several years and even hit number **❶** again with "Hello, I Love You," but their career was about to slam shut, so to speak. In 1971, at age 27, lead singer Jim Morrison was found dead, bloated in a bathtub in a Paris apartment. A rock 'n roll poet with a self-destructive streak, Morrison was grieved by millions of fans - more for his wasted potential than his untimely death. The many "pyro" references Jim sang about in "Light My Fire" have inspired this roasted salad. Grilling the vegetables on the barbecue brings new flavors to otherwise mundane veggies; and the fresh salad dressing enhances the roasted flavors. Will it *set the night on fire*? Well, it'll certainly get it off to a good start.

The Top 9 Ingredients

- 1 large red onion
- 1 head radicchio, quartered through base
- 1 head curly endive, quartered through base
- 1 large head Belgian endive, quartered through base
- ½ lemon
- 6 tablespoons olive oil
- ⅓ cup balsamic vinegar
- ¼ cup chopped fresh basil
- 4 ounces blue cheese, crumbled

Serves 4

Preheat oven to 400°F. Wrap onion in foil. Roast until soft, about 40 minutes. Cool. Peel onion; cut into quarters through stem end. Place onion, radicchio, and endives on baking sheet. Squeeze lemon over. Let stand 30 minutes.

To make dressing, whisk oil, vinegar and basil in bowl. Season with salt and pepper.

Prepare barbecue and heat to high or preheat broiler. Grill onions and endives and radicchio until slightly charred, turning often, about 4 minutes. Place on platter. Drizzle dressing over. Sprinkle with blue cheese and serve. *Hello, I love this salad!*

"To Sirloin, With Love"

Lulu

Her nickname was "the Scottish Brenda Lee." And although she may have been little in size and years, Lulu was certainly BIG when it came to hit records in 1967. The teenager starred in the movie, "To Sir, With Love," with Sidney Poitier and got to sing the title song to boot. When Epic Records released the record, however, the tune was relegated to the "B" side, the "A" being "The Boat That I Row," written by that struggling New York songwriter for the Monkees, what's-his-name...Neil Diamond. Disc jockeys and movie fans couldn't be fooled, though; the "B" side soared and, eventually, "To Sir, With Love" became the **number ❶** hit record of the year. Lulu was married briefly to rock 'n roller Maurice Gibb of the Bee Gees. Like her height, Lulu's rock 'n roll career may have been on the short side, but she's had a long and steady theatrical career in London's West End. The song and movie have now inspired this sirloin steak in a rich and creamy sauce. One taste and you'll agree...it's a *lulu!*

The Top 11 Ingredients

Sauce

- 2 tablespoons olive oil
- ¼ cup minced shallots
- 2 tablespoons minced garlic
- ½ cup dry white wine
- 2 tablespoons Dijon mustard
- 1 cup whipping cream
- ⅔ cup canned beef broth

Steaks

- 2 12-ounce top sirloin steaks (1-inch thick), fat trimmed
- 1 tablespoon cracked black peppercorns
- 1 tablespoon olive oil
- ¼ cup minced fresh parsley

Serves 4

For Sauce

Heat olive oil in medium saucepan over medium heat. Add shallots and garlic; sauté about 3 minutes. Add wine. Increase heat to high and boil until liquid is reduced by half, about 4 minutes. Whisk in mustard, then cream and broth. Boil until reduced to 1¼ cups, about 7 minutes.

For Steaks

Coat both sides of each steak with peppercorns. Season steaks with salt. Heat olive oil in large skillet over medium-high heat. Add steaks to skillet; cook to desired doneness, about 4 minutes per side for rare. Transfer to platter. Add sauce mixture to skillet; bring to boil, scraping up any browned bits. Boil until reduced to 1 cup, about 1 minute. Stir in parsley. Season sauce with salt and pepper. Spoon over steaks.

"Parsley, Sage, Rosemary and Thyme" Pesto

Simon and Garfunkel

Remember the song, "Hey, Schoolgirl," by Tom and Jerry back in '57? In all fairness, not many people do, but that duo (no, not the MGM cartoon stars) eventually changed back to their original names, Simon and Garfunkel - and we certainly remember them. Their albums are considered classics and they hit number ❶ with three singles: "Sounds of Silence," "Mrs. Robinson," and "Bridge Over Troubled Water." When Tom and Jerry, or rather, Simon and Garfunkel separated professionally in 1970, the same year as the Beatles, the sense of loss that music fans felt was enormous. Granted, there would be new musical directions from the individuals, but fans knew there was something magical about the pairings and groupings. Now for rock 'n roll trivia: "Parsley, Sage, Rosemary and Thyme" are lyrics from what Simon and Garfunkel song? But the bigger question is: do these four herbs really go together? The answer is: yes, when put together in the correct proportions. This pesto is a delectable alternative to traditional basil pesto, especially when used in imaginative ways. Oh yeah, and the answer to the other question: "Scarborough Fair/Canticle."

Makes 2 cups

Place first 7 ingredients in food processor and chop finely. With machine running, gradually add ½ cup olive oil. Continue processing until pesto is smooth. Season to taste with salt and pepper.

The Top 8 Ingredients

1½	cup loosely packed fresh parsley
½	cup loosely packed thyme
⅛	cup fresh rosemary leaves
1	teaspoon ground sage
½	cup grated Parmesan cheese
2	garlic cloves
½	cup pine nuts, toasted
½	cup olive oil

Chef Rex-ommendation!

Pesto goes best-o with the following...

- Mix it with olive oil and serve on cooked pasta

- As a condiment on grilled chicken, steaks or chops

- Spread on crackers, served as an hors d'oeuvre

"Purple Glaze"
Jimi Hendrix Experience

The Jimi Hendrix Experience was a short experience. Some questioned his logic, but in the mid-'60s, the Seattle guitarist moved to England to form a band in order to gain recognition here in the U.S. The strategy worked. There, Hendrix caught the eye of the touring tv group, The Monkees, and they asked the Experience to be their opening act back home. Hendrix and the Monkees!?! Talk about a recipe of vinegar and water! The guitar demolishing antics of Hendrix were lost on the Monkee's teeny bopper crowd. Eventually, Hendrix found his own crowd as he continued to smash guitars while making smash hit records, such as "Foxy Lady," "All Along The Watchtower," and "Purple Haze." Jimi's experience with drugs, however, led to a lethal overdose at the age of 27. In his memory, it's time to experience "Purple Glaze." The eggplant provides the purple coloration and it's a terrific relish to serve with fish, chops, steak, or as a side dish. Serve it to your *foxy lady*!

The Top 10 Ingredients

1	1-pound eggplant
1	green bell pepper
1	red bell pepper
3	tablespoons olive oil
¾	cup chopped onion
1	teaspoon minced garlic
1	cup chopped plum tomatoes
½	teaspoon sugar
	dried crushed red pepper
3	tablespoons chopped cilantro
1	tablespoon balsamic vinegar

Makes 1 quart

Preheat oven to 450°F. Pierce eggplant with knife in several places. Place in roasting pan; bake until tender, about 1 hour. Cool slightly. Halve eggplant; scrape out pulp and chop finely.

Char peppers over gas flame or in broiler until blackened on all sides. Wrap in paper bag and let stand 10 minutes. Peel, seed and finely chop peppers.

Heat oil in large skillet over medium-low heat. Add onion; sauté 5 minutes. Add garlic; stir 1 minute. Add tomatoes, sugar and pinch of red pepper. Increase heat to medium-high; stir until thick, about 5 minutes. Add eggplant, bell peppers and cilantro; bring to simmer. Reduce heat to low, cover and cook until thick, stirring often, about 30 minutes. Cool to room temperature.

Stir vinegar into relish. Cover; chill overnight.

(Take Another Little) "Piece Of My Tart"

Janis Joplin

Pearl was her nickname. But the gravel throated, hard-drinking, rock 'n roll mama was better known as Janis Joplin. The rowdy, bawdy Texan was a far cry from the sweet girls like Shelley Fabares, Brenda Lee and Lulu who also inhabited the music charts during the '60s. Performing with Big Brother and the Holding Company, Janis wailed on the record (Take Another Little) "Piece Of My Heart," from the album "Cheap Thrills." Despite its success, Janis quit the band to form one of her own, Full Tilt Boogie. Together they recorded the album "Pearl," which produced Pearl's only **number ❶** hit, "Me and Bobby McGee." It was a success she was never to savor, unfortunately. Like rockers Jim and Jimi (Morrison and Hendrix), Janis was found dead of a drug overdose. All three died at the age of 27. But enough about tragedy - Janis was all about cheap thrills, which is exactly what you'll get from this tart named for her song. It's delicious right out of the oven or served cold the next day. Janis would have enjoyed it along with a bottle of Southern Comfort, but that option will be left up to you.

The Top 10 Ingredients

2	tablespoons (¼ stick) butter
1	medium onion, thinly sliced
⅓	cup diced green bell pepper
4	ounces ham, diced
1	teaspoon herbs de Provence
1	refrigerated pie crust
2	cups whipping cream
5	large eggs
½	teaspoon salt
¼	teaspoon pepper

Serves 6

Preheat oven to 425°F. Melt butter in large skillet over medium-high heat. Add onion and diced bell pepper and sauté until golden brown, stirring occasionally, about 8 minutes. Add ham and herbs de Provence and sauté 1 more minute. Season to taste with salt and pepper. Transfer to bowl and cool.

Line 9-inch glass pie dish with crust. Crimp edges decoratively. Arrange onion and ham mixture in crust. Whisk cream, eggs, salt and pepper in large bowl to blend. Pour mixture into crust.

Bake at 425°F for 15 minutes then reduce heat to 300°F and bake for approximately 30 minutes or until custard is set and begins to brown. Transfer to rack and cool 10 minutes. Serve, but save enough for *Me and Bobby McGee.*

"Jumpin' Jackcheese In a Flash" Sandwiches

The Rolling Stones

They're known as the "Bad Boys of Rock 'n Roll." It's a reputation they've worked hard for, are proud of, and best of all - after all these years - the Stones are still rolling. Mick Jagger, Keith Richards, and the others have charted consistently for 4 decades now, chalking up 7 **number ❶** singles, and countless other rock 'n roll classics. Next to the Beatles, the Stones had the biggest influence on rock 'n roll during the '60s, but unlike the Fab Four, they're still going strong today. "Jumpin' Jack Flash" is a favorite that fans and *honky tonk women* expect to hear at a Stone's concert, which still draw record crowds to this day. "Jumpin' Jackcheese in a Flash" Sandwiches are as good as the Stones are bad. If you *can't get no satisfaction* from the sandwiches you've made in the past, *start me up* one of these today. "Jumpin' Jackcheese in a Flash" Sandwiches are a *gas, gas, gas*!

The Top 6 Ingredients

- 4 slices whole grain bread
- 4 tablespoons "Be-Bop-A-Lula" Sauce (see page 15)
- 1 small red onion, thinly sliced
- 6 ounces sliced smoked turkey breast
- 1 avocado, peeled, thinly sliced
- 1 cup grated hot pepper Monterey Jack cheese

Serves 2

Preheat broiler. Place bread on baking sheet. Spread 1 tablespoon "Be-Bop-A-Lula" Sauce on each slice of bread. Top each with onion slices, turkey and avocado. Sprinkle open-faced sandwiches with cheese. Broil until cheese melts and bubbles. Serve immediately. Careful with the "Be-Bop-A-Lula" sauce or you'll end up with *sticky fingers*!

"Corn To Be Wild"

Steppenwolf

John Kay figured he may as well take a shot at rock 'n roll - once the East Germans had finished taking their shots at him. As a young man, Kay escaped from East Berlin to West at gunfire. Years later, free to pursue what he wanted, he and fellow musicians put together the rock group Steppenwolf, taking the name from the novel of the same by German writer, Herman Hesse. "Born To Be Wild" was their breakthrough hit and is considered by many to be the greatest rock 'n roll motorcycle song ever (as witness in the motorcycle movie classic, "Easy Rider," with Peter Fonda and Dennis Hopper). The group's single, "Magic Carpet Ride," also made the Top 5 in '68, but by '72 most of the magic was gone. The band broke up, but not before their label, Dunhill, had managed to collect some $40 million in worldwide sales - not a bad ride at all. Now's the time to hop on your motorcycle to go buy the ingredients for "Corn To Be Wild." It's a fresh, tasty vegetable side dish - and if it doesn't give your tongue a *magic carpet ride* to new flavors, nothing will.

The Top 10 Ingredients

3	ears fresh corn with husks
1	large fresh green chilies
1	small red bell pepper
1	shallot, minced
½	cup sliced green onions
½	cup chopped red onion
¼	cup chopped fresh cilantro
3½	tablespoons fresh lime juice
1½	tablespoons olive oil
3	garlic cloves, minced

Serves 4

Place corn in large bowl of ice water and let soak 3 hours.

Prepare barbecue and heat to medium-high. Roast corn until husks are charred, turning often, about 10 minutes. Shuck corn. Cut corn from cob.

Meanwhile, char green chili and red bell pepper on grill until blackened on all sides. Seal in paper bag and let stand 10 minutes. Peel, seed and chop each.

Combine corn, chilies, red bell pepper and remaining ingredients in large bowl and stir. Season with salt and pepper. Is this corn wild...or what!?

"Classical Gas" Baked Beans

Mason Williams

Extremely rare - that term not only applies to grilled steaks, but how often an instrumental record has climbed the charts during the rock 'n roll era. "Classical Gas" had the octane to do just that, however. Musician Mason Williams was a regular performer on the hit tv series, "The Smothers Brothers Comedy Hour." The show also developed the talents of White House hopeful Pat Paulsen, and an up-and-coming comic with an arrow through his head, Steve Martin. Williams performed his hit record, "Classical Gas," on the show, and now it's time for you to perform "Classical Gas" Baked Beans in the kitchen. It's a hearty, three bean side dish. One taste and you'll understand it's "classical" status. Then wait a few hours and you'll understand the reference to "gas."

The Top 14 Ingredients

- 1 pound ground pork sausage
- 1 teaspoon fennel seed
- 1 teaspoon fresh thyme
- 1 medium onion, chopped
- 1 green bell pepper, chopped
- 1 can white beans, drained (Great Northern)
- 1 can kidney beans, drained
- 1 can pinto beans, drained
- 1 small can tomato paste
- 1 can beef broth
- ⅓ cup brown sugar
- 1 teaspoon dry mustard
  dash Worcestershire sauce

Serves 8

In large skillet, sauté ground pork sausage. After sausage is browned, add fennel seed and thyme and continue to sauté until crispy and flavorful. Remove from pan; drain on paper towel. In remaining pan drippings sauté onion and bell pepper until tender, about 5 minutes.

Preheat oven to 250°F. In large baking dish, combine sausage, onion, bell pepper and all remaining ingredients and stir. Salt and pepper to taste. Cover and bake in a slow oven for 4 to 6 hours. Serve while hot. Wait another 4 to 6 hours and open windows to allow *"classical gas"* to escape.

Chef Rex-ommendation!

For classier results - bake "Classical Gas" Baked Beans in presoaked clay roaster. Place in cold oven, turn oven on at 250°F, cook for 4 to 6 hours.

"I Stuffed It Through The Grape Vine"

Marvin Gaye

Psst! You didn't hear it here...but rumor has it that Motown records had a hit time and time again with "I Heard It Through The Grape Vine." In '68, Marvin Gaye spent 7 weeks in the number ❶ position with the song, making it the second biggest hit of the year (right after The Beatles' "Hey, Jude"). The previous year "...Grape Vine" had been a big hit for Gladys Knight and the Pips, placing at number 9 for the year - making it the only song to ever place in the yearly Top 10 for two consecutive years. Smokey Robinson and the Miracles, the Isley Brothers, the Temptations, and Undisputed Truth have also recorded it, albeit with lesser success. So you want a hit record? Then I'd suggest you record this song - right after you make this namesake recipe. These stuffed grape leaves are the perfect hors d'oeuvre to serve before a rock 'n roll dinner party. Don't take my word for it though - chances are you'll *hear it through the grapevine,* too.

The Top 13 Ingredients

6	tablespoons olive oil
1	onion, chopped
1/3	cup wild rice
1/3	cup brown rice
1/2	teaspoons ground allspice
1 1/2	cups water
1/4	cup golden raisins, chopped
1	chicken bouillon cube
1/4	cup pine nuts
1	8-ounce jar grape leaves, drained (available at Greek & Italian markets)
1/4	cup water
1/4	cup fresh lemon juice
	fresh lemon wedges
1/2	cup chopped fresh parsley

Serves 12...or 2 hungry people

Heat 2 tablespoons oil in medium saucepan over medium heat. Add onion and sauté until tender, about 5 minutes. Add rices and allspice and stir 1 minute. Add 1 1/2 cups water and chopped raisins and bring to boil. Add chicken bouillon cube, reduce heat to low, cover, and simmer until water is absorbed and rice is tender, about 20 minutes. Remove from heat.

Toast pine nuts in broiler or toaster until until golden. Add to rice mixture. Season with salt and pepper.

Bring large pot of water to boil. Add grape leaves and stir to separate. Turn off heat; let stand 1 minute. Drain. Rinse with cold water to cool; drain well.

Cover bottom of large skillet or Dutch oven with about 10 grape leaves, pressing about 1 inch up sides of skillet. Arrange 1 leaf, vein side up, on work surface. Place 1 rounded tablespoon rice filling near stem. Fold in sides, then roll up jelly roll fashion. Repeat with remaining filling and leaves. Arrange stuffed leaves, seam side down, close together in leaf-lined skillet. Drizzle 3 tablespoons olive oil over. Add $\frac{1}{4}$ cup water and fresh lemon juice and bring to boil. Reduce heat to medium-low, cover and cook about 50 minutes. Cool completely.

Arrange stuffed grape leaves on platter. Garnish with lemon and parsley and serve to guests with this song playing in the background - either the Gaye version, or Gladys Knight - or your own karaoke version!

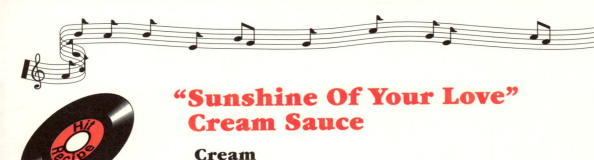

"Sunshine Of Your Love" Cream Sauce

Cream

Cream rises to the top, goes the old cliche. So it's only fitting that Ginger Baker, Jack Bruce, and Eric Clapton called themselves Cream. The trio formed their band in '67 and generated a lot of buzz around rock circles since they were considered to be the cream of the rock 'n roll crop. Although the boys played together for three brief years (Cream curdled fast, one might say), they left behind the albums "Disraeli Gears," "Wheels of Fire," and "Fresh Cream," among others. Their single, "Sunshine Of Your Love," was a big hit in the summer of '68, and now this cream sauce bears its name. Go to the kitchen, get your *disraeli gears* into action, and make this "Sunshine" sauce. It's so easy, so good - see if this *cream* recipe doesn't rise to the top of your list.

The Top 10 Ingredients

- 8 ounces cream cheese, cut into pieces
- 1 cup pine nuts, toasted
- 1 large fresh cilantro bunch, stemmed
- 1 large fresh parsley bunch, stemmed
- ½ cup grated Parmesan cheese
- ¼ cup fresh lime juice
- ¼ cup vegetable oil
- 1 teaspoon pepper
- ¼ teaspoon cayenne pepper
- ¼ cup whipping cream

Makes about 2 cups

Combine first 9 ingredients in blender or food processor. Process until smooth. Transfer to medium bowl. Whisk in cream. Season to taste with salt. Heat sauce in medium saucepan over low heat until warmed before serving.

Chef Rex-ommendation!

Cream Sauce becomes a Dream Sauce when served over...

- grilled chicken
- cooked pasta
- steamed or grilled vegetables

"Proud Marys"

Creedence Clearwater Revival

Groupies, fans, and disc jockeys affectionately called the record-makers CCR, but their real name, for the record, was Creedence Clearwater Revival. Their "rock 'n roll-meets-bijou-blues-sound" had most fans convinced they hailed from Louisiana, when in fact they originated from the San Francisco bay area. Led by brothers John and Tom Fogerty, the band had a clear string of hits in the late '60s, including "Bad Moon Rising," "Green River" and "Fortunate Son." Not so fortunate is the fact that none of their songs ever reached number one, although they hit number two just about every time out. "Proud Mary" is CCR's rock 'n roll classic, one that Ike and Tina Turner remade two years later. What makes these Marys so proud are the tasty ice cubes. No mere clearwater in these cubes, these contain tomato juice and spices. Careful, though...a few of these "Proud Marys" and you'll be *rolling down the river!*

The Top 10 Ingredients

4 cups tomato juice
6 tablespoons fresh lemon juice
3 tablespoons fresh lime juice
2 teaspoons Tabasco sauce
4 teaspoons Worcestershire sauce
1 teaspoon garlic salt
1 tablespoon celery salt
1 teaspoon prepared horseradish
¾ cup vodka
1 zucchini, cut in 4 lengths

Serves 4

Combine 1 cup tomato juice, 2 tablespoons lemon juice, 1 tablespoon lime juice and 1 teaspoon Tabasco sauce. Pour into ice cube tray; freeze overnight to create "Proud Marycles."

Combine Worcestershire sauce, garlic salt, celery salt, horseradish and remaining 3 cups tomato juice, 4 tablespoons lemon juice, 2 tablespoons lime juice and 1 teaspoon Tabasco in pitcher. Stir; add vodka, stir well. Divide "Proud Marycles" among 4 tall glasses. Pour tomato juice mixture over. Garnish each glass with 1 zucchini slice and serve 'em *proudly!*

"In A Gadda Da Vida" Salsa
on Iron Butterflied Shrimp

What name is both 'heavy' and 'light'? Back in '66, that was the question several San Diego rock 'n rollers were asking themselves as they tried to name their band. Eventually, they decided Iron Butterfly. A one night gig at the Los Angeles nitery, The Whiskey A-Go-Go, turned into a 3 week stay for the band...and record contracts followed. "In A Gadda Da Vida" (The Garden of Eden) was their biggest hit record, and a 17 minute one at that! The song was almost longer than their rock 'n roll career, as the Butterfly collapsed in '71. And whatever happened to the band members!? Funny you should ask - for a few years ago a balding, potbellied butcher in a delicatessen, not far from the Whiskey A-Go-Go, confessed that he was an ex-Iron Butterflier. From rock 'n roll star to deli butcher...ain't rock 'n roll grand?? Rest assured this butterflied shrimp recipe is. Like the group's name, the taste is 'heavy,' but the shrimp 'light.'

The Top 19 Ingredients

Stock

- 1 tablespoon olive oil
- 1 large tomato, chopped
- 1 leek, chopped
- 1 celery stalk, chopped
- ½ carrot, chopped
- 1 large shallot, chopped
- 1 tablespoon tomato paste
- 4 cups water
- ¼ cup dry white wine
- 2 tablespoons brandy
  parsley sprigs

"In A Gadda Da Vida" Salsa

- 2 large tomatoes, diced
- ½ cup olive oil
- ¼ cup balsamic vinegar
- 2 teaspoons chopped fresh thyme
- 1½ teaspoons chopped fresh rosemary
  pinch of saffron threads

Iron Butterflied Shrimp

- 1 pound uncooked large shrimp, peeled, deveined
- 2 tablespoons olive oil
- 2 tablespoons finely chopped shallots
- 2 tablespoons fresh chopped parsley
- 2 large garlic cloves, minced
- 2 tablespoons brandy
- 1 teaspoon fresh lemon juice
- 5 tablespoons butter
- ¼ cup chopped fresh chives or green onions

Serves 4

For Stock

Heat olive oil in large saucepan over medium heat. Add tomato, leek, celery, carrot and shallot. Mix in tomato paste. Add 4 cups water, wine, brandy and parsley. Boil until liquid is reduced to $\frac{1}{2}$ cup, about 1 hour. Strain. Cover and chill.

For "In A Gadda Da Vida" Salsa

Preheat oven to 300°F. Combine all ingredients in baking dish, stir, and bake 30 minutes. Drain off liquid and reserve for another use. Portion out "In A Gadda Da Vida" Salsa onto 4 plates.

For Iron Butterflied Shrimp

Butterfly shrimp by slicing down the center (but not all the way through!) and spreading open, butterfly-like. Heat oil in large skillet over high heat. Add shallots, parsley and garlic and sauté 1 minute. Add shrimp and cook about 2 minutes. Pour brandy over; simmer 1 minute. Using slotted spoon, place shrimp atop "In A Gadda Da Vida" Salsa. Add $\frac{1}{2}$ cup stock and lemon juice to skillet. Boil until liquid is reduced to $\frac{1}{3}$ cup, about 2 minutes. Whisk in butter. Stir in chives. Season with salt and pepper. Pour sauce over shrimp and serve in either your garden patio...or Gadda Da Vida - it doesn't matter!

"Hair"

Cowsill Custard

Blame Bud Cowsill for all those reruns of "The Partridge Family." A retired Chief Petty Officer, Cowsill had 7 kids to feed and was in debt a hundred grand when record producers finally gave him the break he was looking for - a recording contract for his singing household. The family had their first big hit in '67 with "The Rain, The Park, and Other Things." Its success, in turn, sent tv producers racing off to the networks to sell the concept of "a rock 'n roll family." Shortly thereafter, we had "The Partridge Family." (Now my question: couldn't those savvy producers have convinced Bud to change that name!?...the Window Sills...the Beverly Sills...anything but the *Cowsills*)! Meanwhile, Broadway had it's biggest rock 'n roll musical hit with "Hair." The show generated hits by various artists, including "Aquarius/Let The Sunshine In," "Easy To Be Hard," and the Cowsills' version of the title song. The 'hair' in this dish is nothing to get grossed out about - it's angel hair pasta. The Cowsills' name readily suggests dairy products - so put the ingredients together and you've got this savory entree. It's easy to make, too, so let down your *hair* and give it a try.

The Top 6 Ingredients

- 1 cup whipping cream
- 3 large eggs
- 1 teaspoon minced fresh thyme
- ½ teaspoon ground nutmeg
- 1 cup grated Parmesan cheese
- 3 ounces angel hair pasta, freshly cooked

Serves 8

Preheat oven to 350°F. Butter eight ½ cup soufflé dishes. Whisk first 4 ingredients in medium bowl to blend. Season generously with salt and pepper. Stir in ⅔ cup Parmesan cheese. Divide cooked pasta evenly among prepared soufflé dishes. Pour egg mixture over angel hair pasta. Sprinkle each dish with remaining ⅓ cup Parmesan cheese. Bake until "Hair" custards are set and golden brown, about 20 minutes. Run small sharp knife around sides of soufflé dishes to loosen. Unmold and serve.

Chef Rex-ommendation!

To get "Hair" tingling results, top each custard with a dollop of either...

- "Parsley, Sage, Rosemary and Thyme" Pesto (see page 62)
- "Sunshine Of Your Love" Cream Sauce (see page 70)

"My Cherry Amour" Sauce
on Stevie Wonderbread Pudding

Ever wonder why Stevie Wonder is considered a wonder? He was just a wunderkind of 12 when he recorded his first Motown hit, the wonderful "Fingertips, Pt. II." Since then he's reached the top of the charts 9 times, not to mention his countless other hits. Several albums, including "Innervisions" and "Songs In The Key Of Life," are considered classics and his biggest hit single, "I Just Called To Say I Love You," even won the Oscar in '84. No wonder Wonder is a wonder. "My Cherie Amour" was Stevie's biggest hit in '69, and it seems just desserts to include "My Cherry Amour" as a topping to Stevie Wonderbread pudding. It's a wonderful dessert dedicated to the sweet sounds given to us year after year, decade after decade by Mr. Wonder.

The Top 14 Ingredients

Stevie Wonderbread Pudding

- 2 cups milk
- 1 cup whipping cream
- 3 large eggs
- 3 large egg yolks
- ½ cup brown sugar
- ¼ cup brandy
- 1 teaspoon vanilla extract
- 6 cups white bread cubes, crusts trimmed

"My Cherry Amour" Sauce

- ½ cup whipping cream
- 3 tablespoons sugar
- 2 tablespoons kirsch or cherry brandy
- 4 ounces semisweet chocolate, chopped
- 1 tablespoon unsalted butter
- ¼ cup dried tart cherries, chopped

Serves 8

For Stevie Wonderbread Pudding

Preheat oven to 350°F. Butter 13x9x2-inch glass baking dish. Heat milk and cream in saucepan over medium heat to simmer. Whisk eggs, yolks, brown sugar, brandy and vanilla in large bowl until blended. Gradually whisk in hot milk mixture. Place bread cubes in prepared dish. Pour milk and egg mixture over. Stir until bread is evenly coated. Bake until golden brown and set, about 40 minutes. Remove from oven; cool slightly.

For "My Cherry Amour" Sauce

Bring whipping cream, 3 tablespoons sugar and 2 tablespoons kirsch to boil in small saucepan, stirring to dissolve sugar. Remove from heat; whisk in chocolate and butter. Stir until chocolate melts and is smooth. Whisk in dried cherries. Serve over Stevie Wonderbread Pudding in parfait glasses.

"Give Pizza A Chance"

John Lennon and the Plastic Ono Band

Remember that scandalous nude photo of John and Yoko on their album cover, "Two Virgins"? In hindsight (and their *hinds* were quite a *sight*!), the shocking photo probably instigated more sales at work-out spas than record stores (those scrawny bodies were motivation to go beef up). The album also should have tipped off the public as to the imminent breakup of the Beatles. After all, John and Yoko were obviously busy with their own itinerary. In May of '69, the couple staged their infamous "peace lie-in" in Montreal. The following month, hoping for global unity and tranquility, they recorded "Give Peace A Chance." Ironically, the ambitious Lennon/Ono tune didn't do as well on the music charts as did the Beatles satiric look at the couple, "The Ballad Of John and Yoko." The ballad contains Lennon singing the now hauntingly prophetic lyrics, "...they're gonna crucify me." Tonight, make a peace offering to your loved ones by making this authentic, homemade, heavenly pizza. Sure, it's easier to pick up the phone and order out, but *all we are saying is give pizza a chance.*

Serves 4

For Pizza Sauce
Blanch tomatoes in large pot of boiling water 1 minute. Drain. Peel, seed and chop tomatoes. Transfer to bowl. Mix in remaining ingredients. Makes about 3 cups.

For Pizza Dough
Place 2 tablespoons warm water in bowl. Add sugar and yeast; stir to dissolve. Let stand until foamy, 6 minutes. Mix 1¼ cups all purpose flour, semolina flour and salt in another bowl. Gradually mix in remaining ½ cup plus 2 tablespoons water. Add oil and stir until well blended, about 2 minutes. Using rubber spatula, fold in yeast mixture. Mix in ¾ cup flour (dough will be soft). Turn dough out onto lightly floured surface and knead until smooth and elastic, adding more flour if very sticky, about 7 minutes.

Grease medium bowl. Add dough, turning to coat entire surface. Cover bowl with damp kitchen towel. Let rise in warm draft-free area until doubled in volume, about 1 hour. Punch dough down.

The Top 23 Ingredients

Pizza Sauce
- 1½ pound tomatoes
- ¾ cup tomato purée
- 2 tablespoons fresh chopped basil
- 2 teaspoons minced garlic
- 1 teaspoon salt
- ½ teaspoon pepper
- 1 teaspoon fresh oregano, chopped
- dash of crushed red peppers

Pizza Dough
- ½ cup plus 4 tablespoons warm water (110°F to 115°F)
- 2 teaspoons sugar
- 1½ teaspoons dry yeast
- 2 cups (or more) all purpose flour
- ¼ cup semolina flour (available at specialty foods stores and Italian markets)
- 1½ teaspoons salt
- 1½ tablespoons olive oil

For Topping and Assembly

Fry sausage in medium skillet over medium heat until cooked through, turning frequently, about 15 minutes. Drain and cool sausages. Cut diagonally into ½-inch-thick slices.

Heat oil in small skillet over medium-high heat. Add garlic and sauté 1 minute. Add sliced mushrooms, olives, pine nuts and sauté 4 minutes. Cool mixture. Grate mozzarella cheese. Cut tomatoes into strips. Set topping ingredients aside.

Position rack in lowest third of oven. Place baking stone, baking tiles or large rimless cookie sheet on rack in oven. Preheat oven to 500°F. Sprinkle 2 tablespoons semolina over pizza peel (a wooden paddle used for transferring bread and pizza into or out of the oven) or over another large rimless cookie sheet.

Flatten dough slightly. Place dough over back of hands and stretch in all directions to form 7-inch round. Roll dough out on floured surface to 12-inch round. Transfer to prepared peel or cookie sheet. Using fingertips, press dough around edge to build slightly raised border. Cover with dry kitchen towel and let stand 10 minutes.

Spread sauce over pizza leaving 1-inch border. Sprinkle mozzarella over sauce. Top with sun-dried tomatoes, then mushroom mixture, herbs, and sausages and mozzarella cheese. Slide pizza off peel or cookie sheet and onto stone or preheated cookie sheet in oven. Bake until pizza is brown on edges and bottom, about 10 minutes. Slide peel under pizza or remove cookie sheet and transfer pizza to work surface. Sprinkle pizza with pepper. Cut into wedges and serve. *Peace,* brother. Pizza, sister?

The Top 23 Ingredients (cont.)

Topping

- 8 ounces hot Italian sausage
- 1 tablespoon olive oil
- 1 small garlic clove, minced
- 4 ounces fresh shiitake or button mushrooms, stemmed, sliced
- ⅓ cup sliced ripe black olives
- ⅓ cup pine nuts
- 8 ounces mozzarella cheese
- 3 oil-packed sun-dried tomatoes, drained

Assembly

- 2 tablespoons semolina flour
- ½ cup Pizza Sauce (see recipe)
- 5 fresh basil leaves, sliced
- 12 fresh oregano leaves
- 1 teaspoon pepper

"Sun King" Crab Cakes & "Mean Mr. Mustard" Sauce

The Beatles

A more appropriate title for the Beatles' album, "Abbey Road," might have been "End Of The Road." When the album was released in late '69, little did Beatle fans know it was the last album effort by John, Paul, George and Ringo. True, the album "Let It Be" was released later, after the announcement of their break up, but it had been recorded earlier. "Abbey Road" featured the number ❶ hits, "Come Together" and "Something." Side two featured a medley of songs, one feeding into the next. Among them, "Sun King" blended into "Mean Mr. Mustard" - and that's how the idea for these recipes was born. These crab cakes and mustard sauce *come together* wonderfully - and when quality crab is used (not imitation) they are *something!*

Serves 6

The Top 16 Ingredients

"Mean Mr. Mustard" Sauce
- 5 tablespoons butter,
- 1/3 cup shallots, minced
- 2 tablespoons white wine vinegar
- 1/3 cup dry white wine
- 1/2 cup whipping cream
- 5 teaspoons whole grain Dijon mustard

"Sun King" Crab Cakes
- 2 tablespoons olive oil
- 2 celery stalks, finely chopped
- 1 medium onion, finely chopped
- 1 pound crabmeat (preferably king crab)
- 2 2/3 cups dry Italian breadcrumbs
- 1/4 cup chopped fresh chives
- 2 tablespoons chopped fresh parsley
- 1/2 cup mayonnaise
- 6 tablespoons all purpose flour
- 3 large eggs
- 2 tablespoons vegetable oil

For "Mean Mr. Mustard" Sauce

Melt 1 tablespoon butter in small skillet over medium-low heat. Add shallots; sauté about 5 minutes. Add white wine vinegar and simmer 1 minute. Add wine and simmer until mixture is reduced to 1/3 cup, about 4 minutes. Add cream; simmer until mixture is reduced to scant 1/2 cup, about 5 minutes. Remove mixture from heat; whisk in remaining 4 tablespoons butter and mustard. Season to taste with salt and pepper. Serve over "Sun King" Crab Cakes.

For "Sun King" Crab Cakes

Heat 2 tablespoons olive oil in large skillet over medium heat. Add celery and onion and sauté until tender, about 5 minutes. Transfer to large bowl. Stir in crabmeat, 2/3 cup Italian breadcrumbs, chopped chives and parsley and 1/2 cup mayonnaise. Season with salt and pepper. Form into 12 small cakes. Arrange cakes on baking sheet.

Place flour in small bowl. Whisk eggs to blend in another small bowl. Place remaining 2 cups breadcrumbs in medium bowl. Coat each crabcake with flour. Dip into beaten egg, then into Italian breadcrumbs, coating completely. Heat 1 tablespoon vegetable oil in large skillet over medium heat. Add crab cakes in batches; cook until golden and heated through, adding more oil as necessary, about 5 minutes per side. Serve "Sun King" Crab Cakes with "Mean Mr. Mustard" Sauce.

"Going Up The Country"
Canned Heat Fondue

There's only one problem here. Rock 'n roll historians will tell you Tommy John-son's old song title inspired the name for the blues/rock 'n roll-band from Los Ange-les, Canned Heat. The problem arises because not many people these days remember Tommy Johnson - nor Canned Heat, for that matter. The group charted several times in the late '60s with songs like "On The Road Again" and "Going Up The Country." Canned Heat cooled fast, however, as happens to so many rock groups. But their name brings to mind cans of sterno...fondue pots...fondue parties...a very communal, late '60s, thing to do. This recipe is a cheese lovers delight. It's so rich and tasty, your heart melts almost as fast as the cheese. So go out to your storage shed, dig out the old fondue pot, buy some *canned heat* (sterno), and dip into this great tasting fondue.

<table>
<tr><td colspan="2">**The Top 7 Ingredients**</td></tr>
<tr><td>9</td><td>ounces swiss cheese, grated</td></tr>
<tr><td>9</td><td>ounces Gruyere cheese, grated</td></tr>
<tr><td>2</td><td>tablespoons flour</td></tr>
<tr><td>1½</td><td>cups dry white wine</td></tr>
<tr><td>1</td><td>tablespoon kirsch (clear cherry brandy)</td></tr>
<tr><td></td><td>ground nutmeg</td></tr>
<tr><td>1</td><td>french bread loaf, cut into 1-inch cubes</td></tr>
</table>

Serves 4-8

Toss cheeses with flour in bowl. Bring dry white wine to simmer in fondue pot or large saucepan over medium heat. Add 1 handful of cheese to pot and whisk until melted and smooth. Repeat with remaining cheese 1 handful at a time, whisking until melted and smooth after each addition. Mix in kirsch and pinch of nutmeg. Season to taste with salt and pepper. Whisk until beginning to bubble, about 2 minutes.

Serve fondue with bread cubes and skewers, allowing diners to skewer and dip bread. Be sure to set fondue pot over *canned heat*.

Chef Rex-ommendation!

Instead of french bread, try cubes of...
- "Make It With You" - Bread (see page 85)
- "Knead You Tonight" - INXS Bread (see page 149)

Recipes of the '70s

"Balls Of Confusion"
the appetizer Temptations

The Temptations were almost as famous for their smooth moves and synchronized motions as they were their hit records. During the '60s, every teenager knew the Temptations' moves as well as their song lyrics. The Motown group had lots of songs, among them four number ❶ hits, "My Girl," "I Can't Get Next to You," "Just My Imagination (Running Away With Me)," and "Papa Was A Rolling Stone." Recorded at the peak of their career, "Ball of Confusion" has now inspired this appetizer - and the confusion will come from your guests. As they nibble, they'll be wondering: is it *just my imagination (running away with me)* or are these *balls of confusion* delicious? Yes, they are! The dried pears and ham confuse the tongue with their unusual yet winning combination of flavors. The *temptation* is to reach for another. Go for it!

The Top 11 Ingredients

1¼	cup all purpose flour
¾	cup yellow cornmeal
3	tablespoons sugar
2½	teaspoons baking powder
½	teaspoon salt
½	cup buttermilk
2	eggs, beaten
6	tablespoons (¾ stick) butter, melted
1¼	cups finely diced ham
1	cup finely diced dried pears (available in specialty stores such as Trader Joe's and Hadleys)
	vegetable oil (for deep frying)

Makes about 36

No need for confusion now...it's easy. Mix first 5 ingredients in large bowl. Add buttermilk, eggs and butter and stir until well combined. Mix in ham and pears. Set aside.

Heat oil in large saucepan to to medium or in deep fryer to 375°F. Carefully spoon ham and pear mixture by rounded tablespoons into oil (do not crowd) and cook until deep golden brown, turning occasionally, about 5 minutes. Transfer "balls" to paper towels using slotted spoon and drain. Repeat with remaining mixture in batches. Transfer to platter.

Chef Rex-ommendation!

For dip temptations try...
- "Be-Bop-A-Lula" Sauce (see page 15)
- "Mean Mr. Mustard" Sauce (see page 78)

"Whole (Wheat) Lotta Love"

Led Zeppelin Rolls

Ever hear of the rock group named "No BS"? In 1974, Baron von Zeppelin threatened to sue the British supergroup if they performed in Copenhagen under the name Led Zeppelin. So rather than cancel, "No BS" performed for thousands of Danish fans while the Danish Baron sat at home alone eating danish pastry - no BS! Led Zeppelin was formed back in '68 when the Yardbirds broke up. Ex-Yardbird guitarist Jimmy Page then joined forces with other heavyweight session players John Paul Jones, Robert Plant and John Bonham. As Led Zeppelin, they soared when their first album went gold and produced the hit single, "Whole Lotta Love." The group broke up in '80 when Bonham was found dead (40 shots of vodka consumed in less than 12 hours - yep, that'll do it)! Plant and Page have since re-teamed with various degrees of success, but the Zeppelin was only flying high during the late '60s and early '70s. Now we have Led Zeppelin Rolls and, like the group, they're considered heavyweights. It's not that they're leaden, they're just heavy because there's a whole lotta wheat in them...and a *whole lotta love*.

The Top 10 Ingredients

1¾	cups whole wheat pastry flour
⅓	cup sugar
1½	teaspoons baking powder
¾	teaspoon baking soda
½	teaspoon salt
¾	cup (1½ sticks) butter, cut into pieces
1⅓	cups rolled oats
½	cup dried raisins
10	tablespoons (or more) buttermilk
1	egg, beaten (glaze)

Makes 2 dozen

Preheat oven to 375°F. Butter cookie sheet. Combine first 5 ingredients in food processor. Add butter and cut in until mixture resembles fine meal. Transfer to large bowl. Mix in oats and raisins. Add 10 tablespoons buttermilk and mix just until dough comes together, adding more buttermilk by tablespoons if dry. Turn dough out onto floured surface. Pat into 1-inch-thick round. Cut out rounds using 3-inch cookie cutter. Gather scraps; pat into 1-inch-thick "zeppelin." Cut out more "zeppelins".

Transfer "zeppelins" to prepared cookie sheet, spacing 3 inches apart. Brush generously with egg glaze. Bake "zeppelins" until brown, about 30 minutes. Cool slightly on rack. Serve warm.

"Make It With You"
Bread

Any way you slice it, Bread had a recipe for success during the summer of '70. The soft rock group put enough talent (or was it yeast!?) in the song "Make It With You" to make it rise to the top of the charts. Led by vocalist David Gates, Bread jammed many a session together and made plenty of dough during the early '70s. However, by '73 the band's career and good fortune had turned to crumbs. David Gates didn't loaf around, though; on his own he had a hit with the title song to the movie, "The Goodbye Girl." Bread's bread represented here is simple, basic, and terrific when served hot from the oven. Need some bread?...then start kneading! (Okay, okay, no more crusty looks, that's the end of these crummy *bread* pans...er, puns).

The Top 7 Ingredients

1	package dry yeast
2	cups warm milk
7	cups buttermilk baking mix (such as Bisquick)
¼	cup sugar
½	teaspoon salt
4	large eggs
¼	teaspoon cream of tartar

Makes 2 loaves

Sprinkle yeast over warm milk in saucepan. Let stand 10 minutes.

Sift baking mix, sugar and salt into large bowl. Whisk eggs and cream of tartar in small bowl. Add milk mixture and egg mixture to dry ingredients; stir. On floured butcherblock cutting board, knead bread until well blended, about 2 minutes. Cover with plastic wrap. Let rise in warm draft-free area until doubled in size, about 1 hour.

Lightly oil two bread loaf pans. Stir down dough. Divide evenly between prepared pans. Cover with plastic wrap. Let dough rise again until double in volume, about 1 hour.

Preheat oven to 350°F. Bake bread until golden brown, about 40 minutes. Transfer pans to racks and cool 10 minutes. Serve warm.

"He Ain't Heavy... He's My Poundcake"

with Hollies Sauce

S uccess is such sweet revenge. The Hollies were *on a carousel* to success in the '60s with hit songs like "On A Carousel," "Bus Stop" and "Carrie-Anne." Then in '68, when member Graham Nash jumped off the carousel, so to speak, by leaving the group to form C.S.N.& Y., many predicted doom for the remaining Hollies. Quite the contrary happened, without Nash the group achieved three of their biggest hits, "Long Cool Woman," "The Air That I Breathe," and this recipe's inspiration, "He Ain't Heavy, He's My Brother." (Rock 'n Roll trivia buffs, take note: playing piano on "...Heavy" was a young, up-and-coming piano player named Reggie Dwight. He would later change his name to Elton John). This poundcake is a pleasant change from other poundcakes, thanks to the tasty, toasted walnuts. And when topped with heavenly Hollies sauce, I'm telling you, it's...*heavy*!

The Top 13 Ingredients

Hollies Sauce

- ¼ cup (½ stick) unsalted butter
- 2 tablespoons pure maple syrup
- 2 tablespoons whipping cream
- 6 tablespoons powdered sugar, sifted

"Heavy...Poundcake"

- 2 cups coarsely chopped walnuts, toasted
- 2¼ cups sifted flour
- 1 teaspoon baking powder
- ½ teaspoon salt
- 1 cup (2 sticks) butter
- 1¼ cups sugar
- 5 large eggs
- ½ cup pure maple syrup
- ¾ teaspoon maple flavoring
- ½ teaspoon vanilla extract

- 12 walnut halves

Serves 12

For Hollies Sauce

Melt butter with maple syrup and cream in small saucepan. Remove from heat. Add powdered sugar and whisk until smooth. Cool glaze until slightly thickened.

For "He Ain't Heavy...He's My Poundcake"

Preheat oven to 350°F. Lightly butter 9x5x3-inch loaf pan. Coarsely chop walnuts in food processor. Toast walnuts and set aside. Sift flour, baking powder and salt into medium bowl. Using electric mixer, beat butter and sugar in large bowl until light and fluffy. Add eggs, beating well. Beat in maple syrup, maple flavoring and vanilla extract (batter may look curdled). Mix in dry ingredients. Fold in chopped toasted walnuts.

Pour batter into prepared loaf pan. Bake until top is golden and toothpick inserted comes out clean, about 1 hour. Transfer pan to rack; cool cake 10 minutes. Turn cake out onto rack and cool completely. Drizzle glaze over pound cake. Arrange walnut halves decoratively on top of cake. Mmmm...*heavy, brothe*r!

"Cinnamon Girls"

Neil Young

How does Neil stay young? He's constantly reinventing himself, constantly keeping himself fresh, constantly delighting new audiences... and old. Over the years, the Canadian rocker has been part of Buffalo Springfield; Crazy Horse; Crosby, Stills, Nash & Young, not to mention his solo career. Most recently he toured with Pearl Jam, which pleased both Generation X and their Baby Boomer parents. Many albums, such as "After The Gold Rush," "Harvest," and "Streets of Angels" are considered classics, thanks to Neil's moody and reflective songs. His single, "Cinnamon Girl," was an upbeat exception. These "Cinnamon Girls" may not have a *"Heart of Gold"* (Neil's biggest hit to date) but they have a toasted pecan right in the heart of the muffin - which is almost as good.

The Top 11 Ingredients

½	cup (1 stick) butter
1	cup firmly packed brown sugar
1	egg
1	teaspoon vanilla extract
1½	cups flour
2	teaspoons baking powder
½	teaspoon baking soda
1	cup buttermilk
⅓	cup granola
½	cup brown sugar
1	teaspoon ground cinnamon
12	toasted pecan halves

Makes 12 rolls

Preheat oven to 350°F. Butter and flour cupcake pan. Using electric mixer, cream butter with 1 cup brown sugar in large bowl until fluffy. Add egg and vanilla and beat until well blended. Sift flour, baking powder and baking soda together; mix into butter alternately with buttermilk, beginning and ending with dry ingredients. Pour into prepared cupcake pan.

Mix ½ cup brown sugar, granola, and cinnamon in small bowl. Place toasted pecan half atop each cupcake. Press each nut 1-inch into batter. Spoon some granola mixture into depressions created by pecans. Sprinkle remaining mixture over each cupcake.

Bake until tester inserted into center comes out clean, about 35 minutes. Cool completely in pan.

"Woodstock" Favorite

Crosby, Stills, Hash and Young Chicken

Here's a recipe for a Super Group: add one part "Byrd" (Crosby), two parts "Buffalo Springfield" (Stills and Young), a dash (or Nash) of "Hollies" and you've concocted Crosby, Stills, Nash and Young. Any time these guys start cooking in the studio together, perfect harmonies and memorable songs are the result. "Woodstock" was an early hit single, a tribute to the landmark-historic-musical-gathering-happening-upper-state-New-York-muddy-thing. This terrific hash recipe honors that song, that group, and what may be remembered as the concert of the century. After all, how many concerts have sequels 25 years later!?

The Top 8 Ingredients

- 2½ pounds red-skinned potatoes, peeled, quartered lengthwise
- 3 tablespoons butter
- 3 onions, chopped
- 4 skinless boneless chicken breasts, cut into ¾-inch pieces
- 2 9-ounce packages frozen artichoke hearts, cooked according to package directions
- 1 cup whipping cream
- 1 cup grated Parmesan cheese
- 2 teaspoons dried tarragon

Serves 6

Cook potatoes in large pot of boiling water until almost tender, about 12 minutes. Drain and cool slightly, then dice.

Place butter in large skillet and melt over medium heat. Add onions and cook until golden brown, stirring occasionally, about 10 minutes. Increase heat to high. Add chicken and potatoes; cook until potatoes are golden brown and chicken is white, stirring frequently, about 6 minutes. Add cooked artichoke hearts, cream, Parmesan cheese and 1 teaspoon tarragon. Boil until cream thickens and coats hash well and chicken is cooked through, stirring frequently, about 3 minutes. Season to taste with salt and pepper. Garnish hash with remaining tarragon, and serve to the *sweet (sic) Judy Blue Eyes* in your life.

"It's Too Late" Easy Potatoes

Carole King

"Oh!" Carol! Back in the late '50s, teeny bopper songwriter Neil Sedaka wrote that song about his girlfriend - and who could've guessed she'd go on to write songs herself and become the most successful female songwriter of all time!? Besides Sedaka, Carole King had other soon-to-be-famous rock 'n roll school chums, including a short kid who teamed with a tall classmate and together they recorded hits like "Bridge Over Troubled Water." With ex-husband Gerry Goffin and on her own, Carole wrote scores of songs, including four that hit **number ❶** for other performers. "It's Too Late" was from Carole's solo album, "Tapestry," a classic which is still selling strong more than 20 years later, having recently passed the 10 million units mark. Hope *it's* not *too late* to say congrats, Carole. It's definitely not too late to make "It's Too Late" Easy Potatoes. They're quick, easy, and *Oh! Carol*, so good!

The Top 6 Ingredients

	olive oil
3	russet potatoes, peeled, thinly sliced
1	medium onion, peeled, thinly sliced
¼	cup grated parmesan cheese
	salt and pepper
¼	cup chopped parsley

Serves 4

Preheat oven to 375°F. Coat bottom of pizza pan with 1 tablespoon olive oil. Layer potato slices around pan. Next, layer onion slices on top of potato slices. Sprinkle parmesan cheese over potatoes and onions. Salt and pepper to taste. Sprinkle chopped parsley on top. Now, drizzle olive oil over potatoes and onions...not too much! Bake for 15-20 minutes, until golden brown. Serve immediately to your dinner guest - and you can be sure...*you've got a friend!*

Chef Rex-ommendation!

It's not too late to serve this tasty 'tator dish with...

- "Love Me Tender"loin (see page 5)
- "To Sirloin, With Love" (see page 61)
- "I'd Do Anything For..." Meatloaf (see page 173)
- "Spanish Harlem" Frittata (see page 28)

"Beginnings"

Chicago

"Beginnings" was the beginning of big stuff for Chicago. In 1971 they saw their first four albums chart at nearly the same time. Originally called Chicago Transit Authority, the group shortened their name when Mayor Richard Daley reportedly threatened a lawsuit. Ironically, the group outlasted Daley. For three decades now these musicians have had hit after hit, including number ❶ smashes, "If You Leave Me Now," "Hard to Say I'm Sorry," and "Look Away." Even the group's mothers can boast - their sons were the first rock group to ever play New York's prestigious Carnegie Hall. Despite losing lead singer Peter Cetera to a solo career and lead guitarist Terry Kath to death, due to a gun cleaning accident, Chicago's *a hard habit to break*. There's no end in sight for the group that started with humble "Beginnings." And now there's "Beginnings," the crab cheesecake appetizer, which is hopefully the *beginnings* of a scrumptious rock 'n roll meal at your house.

The Top 17 Ingredients

Sauce

1	2½ pound cooked crab
4	cups water
1	cup dry white wine
1	onion, chopped
2	carrots, chopped
1	garlic clove, minced
2	tablespoons tomato paste
	fresh parsley sprigs
	fresh thyme sprigs
½	cup whipping cream

Cheesecakes

6	ounces cream cheese
2	large eggs
1	shallot, minced
1	small garlic clove, minced
1½	teaspoons minced fresh dill
1½	teaspoons fresh lemon juice
	cayenne pepper
½	cup (1 stick) chilled butter

Serves 4

For Sauce

Preheat oven to 350°F. Crack crab and remove meat from shells; cover and chill meat until ready to use. Place crab shells in roasting pan. Roast until aromatic, 20 minutes.

Transfer shells to large saucepan. Mix in water, wine, onion, carrots, garlic, tomato paste and herbs and bring to boil. Reduce heat and simmer until liquid is reduced to ½ cup, stirring occasionally, about 1½ hours. Strain. Add cream to cooking liquid and simmer until reduced to ¾ cup, stirring occasionally, about 10 minutes.

For Cheesecakes

Butter four ⅔ cup soufflé dishes. Using electric mixer, beat cream cheese in medium bowl until fluffy. Beat in eggs. Mix in shallot, garlic, dill and lemon juice. Stir in crabmeat. Season to taste with salt, pepper, and cayenne. Divide mixture between dishes. Bake until centers are set, about 30 minutes. Cool slightly.

Run sharp knife around sides of cups to loosen cheesecakes. Invert 1 onto each plate. Bring sauce to simmer. Gradually add butter and whisk until melted. Season to taste with salt, pepper and cayenne. Spoon sauce over cheesecakes and enjoy. Mmmm...so tasty!

"Brown Sugars"
Rolling Stones Cookies

O utrageous! That was the reaction to the Rolling Stone's new logo (the rude red protruding tongue) and to their album cover for "Sticky Fingers," featuring a crotch shot with a real zipper. Both were designed by pop artist Andy Warhol, hired by the Stones in the early '70s as a step to better control their business deals and rock 'n roll destiny. They also formed their own record label and "Brown Sugar" was the bad boys' first single released. It rolled uphill to **number ❶** for the Stones. "Brown Sugars" - the Rolling Stones Cookies are just that - brown sugar and other ingredients rolled up into a stone shaped cookie. They're outrageous, too - outrageously good. You'll have *sticky fingers* reaching for one after another.

The Top 8 Ingredients

1¼	cups packed brown sugar
½	cup (1 stick) unsalted butter
1	large egg
1¾	cups flour
1	teaspoon ground nutmeg
1	teaspoon baking soda
½	teaspoon salt
	sugar

Makes 2 dozen

Using electric mixer, beat brown sugar and butter in bowl until fluffy. Mix in egg. Add flour, nutmeg, baking soda and salt; beat until well blended. Chill 1 hour.

Preheat oven to 350°F. Butter 3 large baking sheets. Roll dough into 1-inch "rolling stones." Roll "stones" in sugar, coating completely. Arrange on prepared baking sheets, spacing "stones" 2 inches apart. Bake until "rolling stones" are golden, about 13 minutes. Cool on baking sheets. Now *Start Me Up* another batch for the freezer.

Chef Rex-ommendation!

Outrageous when served with Madonna's "Espresso Yourself" (see page 153).

"How Can You Mend A Broken Tart?"

Bee Gees

How do you mend a broken singing group? That was the question posed to the Bee Gees in the late '60s. The brothers Gibb were having more sibling rivalry than sibling singing sessions so they disbanded after experiencing moderate success in the mid-'60s. Then Barry Gibb wrote "How Can You Mend A Broken Heart" for singer Andy Williams, who passed on it. (Hey Andy, bet you're the brokenhearted one now.) Consequently, the Bee Gees decided to patch things up and recorded the song themselves. Good thing, too, for it became their first **number ❶** hit - a position they would return to many times, especially during the 'disco craze' of the late '70s. So now the question: how do you mend a broken tart? The answer: you don't, just eat it! Broken into pieces or eaten whole, this tart is a winner - and one that's beautiful to display at dinner parties. Don't be surprised if Andy Williams passes on it, though.

The Top 15 Ingredients

Crust
- 1¾ cups all purpose flour
- ⅓ cup sugar
- 1 tablespoon grated lemon peel
- ½ teaspoon salt
- ¾ cup (1½ sticks) chilled unsalted butter, cut into pieces
- 2 large egg yolks
- 1 tablespoon fresh lemon juice
- 1 teaspoon vanilla extract
- 1 tablespoon (about) water

Filling
- ⅓ cup red currant jelly
- ¼ cup raspberry jam
- 2 tablespoons kirsch (cherry brandy)
- 1 half-pint basket blackberries
- 1 pint fresh strawberries, hulled
- ½ cup fresh blueberries

Serves 6

For Crust
Mix flour, sugar, lemon peel and salt in large bowl. Add butter pieces and blend in using fingertips until mixture resembles coarse meal. Whisk egg yolks, lemon juice and vanilla extract in small bowl to blend. Add to flour mixture and stir until moist clumps from, adding water by tablespoons if mixture is dry. Gather dough into ball and flatten into disk. Wrap dough in plastic and refrigerate 3 hours. That's just enough time to rent the video cassette "Sgt. Pepper's Lonely Hearts Club Band," starring the Bee Gees and George Burns. Perfectly awful, isn't it?

Roll dough out on lightly floured surface to 13-inch round. Transfer dough to 9-inch-diameter tart pan with removable bottom. Press dough onto bottom and up sides; trim edges. Pierce bottom of dough all over with fork. Refrigerate 2 hours - plenty of time to dig out the old "Saturday Night Fever" soundtrack and give it a listen. Still great stuff, huh?

Preheat oven to 425°F. Line crust with aluminum foil. Fill crust with dried beans or pie weights. Bake crust 10 minutes. Remove aluminum foil and dried beans. Bake crust until golden brown, about 20 minutes more, which allows a good opportunity to listen to a few cuts from Streisand's "Guilty" album, which Barry Gibb wrote and produced. Babs was never better, was she? Now then, transfer crust to rack and cool.

For Filling

Cook red currant jelly, raspberry jam and brandy in small saucepan over medium-high heat until thick, stirring frequently, about 3 minutes. Brush some of jam glaze over bottom of tart. Arrange circle of blackberries in ring around inside of tart edge. Arrange strawberries in ring, pointed ends up, inside ring of blackberries. Fill center of tart with blueberries. Brush more jam glaze over all berries. Cut into wedges and serve. Finally, something to eat after this Bee Gees marathon!

"A Raisin To Believe"

Rod Stewart

Rocker Rod has as many hit records as strands of wild hair - and that's a lot! In fact, Stewart is one of the few performers to have had the **number ❶** song of the year on more than one occasion. Once was in '76 with "Tonight's The Night," and the first was in '71 with the double-sided hit, "Maggie May/Reason To Believe." The latter was from the album, "Every Picture Tells A Story," which many rock critics rank as one of the best albums ever recorded. The MTV "unplugged" version of Rod's "Reason..." climbed the charts again in the '90s, so this recipe pays homage to it's double chart entry and classic status. The secret to "A Raisin To Believe" is to eat it when it's completely chilled as the flavors are actually better cold than they are fresh out of the oven. It's easy to make, too, so what're you waiting for?...*tonight's the night*!

The Top 8 Ingredients

¼ cup vanilla ice cream, slightly softened

¼ cup (½ stick) unsalted butter, melted, cooled

½ cup all purpose flour

½ cup apricot jam

½ cup chopped toasted pecans

⅓ cup raisins

⅓ cup golden raisins

milk

Makes 15 slices

Preheat oven to 350°F. Combine ice cream and butter in bowl. Add ½ cup flour; stir until soft dough forms. Coat hands with flour. Shape dough into ball; flatten into disk. Wrap in plastic; freeze until dough is firm, about 15 minutes.

Lightly grease baking sheet. Roll out dough on well-floured surface to 12x16-inch rectangle. Brush dough with jam, leaving ½-inch border at edges. Sprinkle with chopped toasted pecans and raisins. Starting at one long side, roll up dough, jelly roll style. Tuck ends under to enclose filling. Transfer dough to prepared sheet. Using sharp knife, score top of dough into 1-inch sections, then brush with milk.

Bake until golden, about 45 minutes. Run knife under "Raisin To Believe" to loosen from sheet. Cool completely on baking sheet. Slice along score marks. Refrigerate for several hours, until completely cold before serving. *Have I Told You Lately*...how good these are!?

"Garden Party" Salad

Rick Nelson & the Stone Canyon Band

Eric Nelson. Doesn't ring a bell? That's because Eric changed his first name to Ricky and shortly thereafter became a teenaged heartthrob with a string of hit records. Two of those records, "Poor Little Fool" and "Travelin' Man," traveled to **number ❶**. Ten years later, Ricky changed his name again by dropping the "y," and he charted again with "Garden Party." The "garden" reference is Madison Square Gardens where Rick and his backup, The Stone Canyon Band, once played a concert, only to be booed by his fans. To his dismay, Rick realized they wanted him to sing his songs of yesteryear. "Garden Party" was Eric's, Ricky's and Rick's songwriting revenge...and ironically, his biggest hit in a decade. Rick died in a tragic plane crash in '85, but the Nelson music tradition continues via his twin sons, the rockers, "Nelson." This "Garden Party" Salad is a terrific summertime side dish. It's the kind of fresh, flavorful salad you imagine Rick's Mom, Harriett, served to Ozzie and the boys out on the patio after a hard day at the television studio.

The Top 12 Ingredients

Salad

- 2 pounds red-skinned new potatoes
- 1 pound green beans, trimmed
- 1 small red onion, thinly sliced
- 2 green onions, chopped
- ⅓ cup chopped fresh basil
- ¼ cup unsalted sunflower seeds

Dressing

- ¼ cup balsamic vinegar
- 2 tablespoons fresh lemon juice
- 1 garlic clove, minced
  - dash of Worcestershire sauce
- 1 teaspoon herbs de Provence
- ½ cup olive oil

Serves 6

For Salad

In medium saucepan, cover potatoes with water and boil until tender, 10-15 minutes. Cool; cut into quarters. In vegetable steamer, steam green beans until tender, al dente, 5-7 minutes. Drain in cold water. Combine potatoes, green beans, red and green onions and basil in large bowl. Add dressing and stir to coat. Sprinkle with sunflower seeds.

For Dressing

Stir first five ingredients in stainless steel bowl. Slowly dribble in olive oil, whisking gradually. Season to taste with salt and pepper. *Poor little fool* to whoever doesn't like this summer salad!

Chef Rex-ommendation!

Travelin' Men love this served with "Turn, Turn, Turn" - the Byrds on the rotisserie (see page 44).

"American Pie"

Don McLean

A piece of "American Pie" belongs to the history books, for it was the biggest hit record of '72. Singer/songwriter, Don McLean had struggled for years - rejected by 38 record companies - before "Pie" gave him a slice of the music action. The long song (9 minutes plus) paid tribute to McLean's idol, Buddy Holly, with the lyrics "the day the music died" referring to Holly's tragic plane crash. McLean was never able to top the success that "Pie" brought, but it did bring him full circle. In 1988, McLean was asked to sing vocals with the surviving members of Buddy Holly's group, The Crickets, at the Grammy Awards in Radio City Music Hall. Now Don's '72 hit has inspired this pie, which is as American as George Washington and baseball. It has a flavor twist, though, a hearty cornmeal crust. One bite will lead to another...and another...then before long it's *"bye, bye Miss American Pie!"*

The Top 14 Ingredients

Crust

- 2 cups all purpose flour
- ¾ cup yellow cornmeal
- 5 tablespoons sugar
- 1¼ teaspoons pumpkin pie spice
- ½ teaspoon salt
- ¾ cup plus 2 tablespoons solid vegetable shortening, room temperature
- 6 tablespoons (or more) buttermilk

Filling

- 1 cup fresh cranberries
- 1 cup plus 2 tablespoons sugar
- 2 teaspoons pumpkin pie spice
- 3 pounds Pippin apples, peeled, cored, cut into ½-inch-thick slices
- ½ cup dried currants
- 5 tablespoons all purpose flour
  buttermilk

Serves 8

For Crust

Mix first 5 ingredients in food processor. Add shortening and cut in until mixture resembles coarse meal. Blend in enough buttermilk by tablespoons to form dough that begins to clump together. Gather dough into ball; divide in half. Flatten each half into disk. Wrap each disk in plastic and chill 45 minutes.

For Filling

Position rack in lowest third of oven and preheat to 375°F. Coarsely chop cranberries with sugar and pumpkin pie spice in food processor. Transfer mixture to large bowl. Add apples, currants and flour and toss well.

Roll out 1 dough disk between sheets of waxed paper to 13-inch round. Peel off top sheet of paper; invert dough into 9½-inch-diameter deep-dish glass pie dish. Peel off paper. Fold under overhanging dough to form double-thick edge. Roll out remaining dough disk on lightly floured surface to ⅛-inch-thick round. Mound filling in pie dish. Arrange rolled-out pie dough over top. Crimp edges together decoratively. Pierce top of pie with fork, or use sharp knife and cut a decorative design. Brush pastry with buttermilk.

Place pie on baking sheet. Bake 45 minutes. Cover pie with foil and continue baking until juices bubble thickly and crust browns, about 35 minutes more. Transfer pie to rack and cool 1 hour. Serve warm or at room temperature. An American classic, eh?

"An Hors (d'oeuvre) With No Name"

America

Europe might have been a more appropriate name for the trio known as America. The three Americans were raised on overseas military bases and their first **number ❶** hit (and a Top 10 hit for the year), "A Horse With No Name," was about the homesickness they felt for their homeland. Neil Young was hot in the early '70s and his hit, "Heart of Gold," was number one just prior to America's "Horse..." The trio's sound, though, was similar to Young's and many hearing the song for the first time assumed it was Neil's follow up record. Eventually, America established their own sound and hit **number ❶** again in '75 with "Sister Golden Hair," produced by ex-Beatle producer, George Martin. Another hit was "You Can Do Magic" - which is exactly what you can do when you serve this delicious appetizer. "An Hors (d'oeuvre) With No Name" needs no name; it's stuffed mushrooms with wonderful ingredients that speak for themselves.

The Top 10 Ingredients

18	large mushrooms
4	bacon slices
1	tablespoon chopped garlic
1	shallot, minced
1	teaspoon chopped fresh rosemary
$\frac{1}{4}$	cup finely chopped pine nuts
$\frac{1}{4}$	cup chopped olives
1	tablespoon dry Sherry
2	ounces cream cheese, room temperature
	olive oil

Serves 4-6

Remove stems from mushrooms. Coarsely chop stems and set aside. Cook bacon in large skillet over medium heat until crisp. Transfer to paper towels and drain. Pour off all but 1 tablespoon drippings from skillet. Add chopped mushroom stems, garlic, shallot, rosemary, and pine nuts and sauté over medium heat until tender, about 10 minutes. Crumble bacon and add to skillet. Add olives and Sherry and stir to combine until Sherry evaporates. Mix cream cheese in bowl until smooth. Add mushroom mixture and stir to blend. Salt and pepper to taste.

Preheat oven to 375°F. Lightly brush rounded side of mushroom caps with olive oil. Place rounded side down on large baking sheet. Spoon filling into caps, mounding in center. Bake stuffed mushrooms until heated through, about 20 minutes. Transfer mushrooms to platter and serve.

"Truckin' "

Grateful Dead Bread

San Francisco...Haight/Ashbury...flower power...psychedelic rock. Only one rock 'n roll group comes to mind: the great Grateful Dead. (Okay, we'll also toss a bone to Jefferson Airplane, later Starship). Although the Dead seldom charted on the Top 100, they developed a following ("deadheads") that is unparalleled in the rock era. Grateful Dead concert statistics are amazing; the group was constantly a top draw year after year. The Dead kept on *"truckin',"* delighting old deadheads and new generations of deadheads everywhere they went. In '95, when leader Jerry Garcia became one of the dead, literally, "deadheads" showed their love, support, and sympathy by holding candlelight vigils around the world. So make this "Dead" bread, share it with friends, and listen to some Dead music. It makes being a "deadhead" worth living for.

Makes 1 loaf

Stir warm water and honey in large bowl to blend. Sprinkle yeast over. Let stand until foamy, about 8 minutes. Heat buttermilk in small saucepan to lukewarm. Stir into yeast mixture. Add 2 cups bread flour, 2 cups oats, wheat flour, oil and salt and stir until smooth. Gradually mix in enough remaining bread flour to form dough. Cover and let dough rest 15 minutes. Turn out dough onto floured surface. Knead until smooth and elastic, adding more bread flour if sticky, about 10 minutes. Knead in walnuts. Oil large bowl. Add dough; turn to coat. Cover bowl with plastic wrap; let rise in warm, draft-free area until doubled, about 1 hour.

Oil large baking sheet. Punch down dough. Turn out onto oiled surface; knead briefly. Divide dough into 3 pieces. Roll each piece into 16-inch-long rope. Braid ropes together, tuck ends under and pinch to seal. Transfer to prepared sheet. Cover with clean towel. Let rise in warm, draft-free area until almost doubled, about 45 minutes.

Preheat oven to 375°F. Whisk egg and milk in bowl. Brush loaf generously with some of egg mixture. Sprinkle with additional oats. Bake until golden and tester inserted into center comes out clean, about 50 minutes. Transfer to rack; cool.

The Top 12 Ingredients

½ cup warm water
¼ cup honey
1 envelope dry yeast
2 cups buttermilk
4⅓ cups bread flour
2 cups old-fashioned oats
1 cup whole wheat flour
2 tablespoons vegetable oil
2 teaspoons salt
1 cup chopped walnuts
1 egg
2 tablespoons milk
additional old-fashioned oats

"Rocky Mountain High"

John Denver Omelette

During the mid-'70s, John Denver's career was on a high, Rocky Mountain or otherwise. The country boy not only climbed the Rockies, he climbed to the top of the music charts on four occasions, with lesser hits along the way. At the peak of his popularity, Denver was even the spokesman for God...well, at least in the movie, "Oh God," co-starring George Burns as the cigar smoking deity. These days the Aspen, Colorado, singer collects royalty checks and enjoys the mountains he helped make famous. In his honor, we have this John Denver Omelette, which is embellished with fresh herbs, gruyere cheese, and has an easy, folksy flavor. One bite and you'll hum, *Thank God*, (or George Burns) *I'm A Country Boy!*"

Serves 2

The Top 12 Ingredients

- 6 eggs
- 4 teaspoons milk
- 4 teaspoons butter
- ⅓ cup chopped bell pepper
- ⅓ cup onion, chopped
- ⅓ cup ham, minced
- 2 teaspoons chopped fresh parsley
- 2 teaspoons chopped fresh chives
- 2 teaspoons chopped fresh tarragon
- 2 teaspoons chopped fresh thyme
- ⅓ cup grated Gruyere cheese
- sour cream (optional)

Preheat broiler. Whisk eggs and milk in medium bowl. Melt 2 teaspoons butter in large broiler-proof skillet over medium heat. Sauté bell pepper and onion until tender, about 5 minutes. Add ham, herbs and sauté 1 more minute. Add eggs and milk mixture to pan. Cook until eggs are almost set. Sprinkle grated cheese over top and place skillet in broiler until eggs and cheese are golden and fluffy, about 2 minutes. Cut omelette in half, serve immediately. Garnish with dollop of sour cream, if desired.

"You Ain't Seen Nothin' Yet" Slaw
Bachman Turnip Overdrive

No offense, Gary. What turned out to be the biggest hit in Bachman Turner Overdrive's career was never intended to be heard outside the realm of close friends. After the breakup of the successful Canadian group, The Guess Who, the Bachman brothers, Fred and Randy, joined their friend, Fred Turner, and created B.T.O. Randy then wrote and recorded a demo of "You Ain't Seen Nothin' Yet, " a song that poked fun at stuttering and stammering, meant to be a joke for his stuttering brother Gary. Somehow, though, their record producer heard it, liked it, convinced the boys to include it on their next album...and the rest is music chart history. Now there's Bachman *Turnip* Overdrive - and if you aren't convinced that shredded turnips are an interesting alternative to conventional cabbage slaw, then wait 'til you try it. *You ain't seen nothin' yet!*

The Top 8 Ingredients

¾	cup canola oil
⅓	cup red wine vinegar
2	tablespoons Dijon mustard
1	tablespoon fennel seeds
1½	pounds turnips, peeled
2	medium carrots, peeled
1	small red onion
½	cup chopped fresh parsley

Serves 8

In a small bowl, mix red wine vinegar, mustard, and fennel seed. Slowly dribble in the canola oil and whisk until well stirred. Using food processor fitted with grating disk, grate turnips, carrots, and red onion. Place grated vegetables in a large bowl, add dressing, parsley, and toss. Season to taste with salt and pepper. Cover and chill for at least 1 hour before serving. *B-b-b-b-baby, here's a slaw you ain't never gonna forget!*

Chef Rex-ommendation!

You ain't tried nothin' 'til you've tried this slaw with...

- Wham!burgers (see page 143)
- "Yellow Submarines" (see page 49)

"One Of These Delights"

The Eagles

The Eagles were soaring high in '75. "One Of These Nights" was one of those number ❶ hits that made the southern California group so popular. The group helped define the new sound coming from southern California called country rock. Artists like Jackson Brown, J.D. Souther and Linda Ronstadt were making it big in the new genre, but it was Linda's backup band who achieved the greatest success. They branched out on their own and called themselves the Eagles. The group, led by Don Henley and Glenn Frey, had five number ❶ hits during the '70s, and their "Greatest Hits" album is the second bestselling album of all time, just short of Michael Jackson's monster seller, "Thriller." The five strong willed country rockers called it quits in '80, though, with Henley claiming he'd only perform with the Eagles again "when hell froze over." Well, frost must've covered the inferno in '94 because the boys decided a reunion tour was in order. *One of these nights* you ought to make "One Of These Delights." Perhaps if the Eagles had sat down and talked out their differences over a plate of these delightful appetizers, they never would have broken up in the first place.

The Top 10 Ingredients

9	ounces soft fresh goat cheese (such as Montrachet)
9	ounces cream cheese
⅓	cup minced oil-packed sun-dried tomatoes
¼	cup pine nuts, minced
2	tablespoons minced fresh parsley
2	tablespoons minced fresh oregano
12	frozen phyllo pastry sheets, thawed
⅓	cup olive oil
1	large plum tomato, seeded, diced fresh oregano sprigs

Makes about 60 slices

Preheat oven to 375°F. Stir first 6 ingredients in bowl until smooth. Season filling with pepper.

Place 1 phyllo sheet on work surface (keep remainder covered). Brush lightly with olive oil and season with pepper. Top with 1 more phyllo sheet. Brush lightly with oil and season with pepper. Repeat with 1 more sheet. Fold stacked phyllo in half lengthwise. Brush top with olive oil.

Spoon ¼ of filling in 1-inch-wide log down 1 long side of sheet, leaving 1-inch borders. Fold each short end over filling. Brush edges with olive oil. Roll up into log starting at long side. Brush "delight" lightly with olive oil. Press seam to seal. Wrap "delight" tightly in plastic wrap. Refrigerate seam side down. Repeat with remaining phyllo and filling, forming 4 "delights" total. Lightly oil cookie sheets. Place "delights" on prepared sheets, seam sides down. Using sharp knife, score each "delight" (cutting through phyllo only), making 14 diagonal cuts in each. Brush "delights" with oil. Bake until golden, about 15 minutes. Cool 10 minutes. Cut through score lines, forming slices. Arrange cut side up on platter. Garnish slices with tomato and oregano.

"Fame"

David Bowie-tie Pasta

Rock fame, movie fame, theatre fame...David Bowie knows a thing or two about fame. His song "Fame" was co-written with a famous ex-Beatle married to Yoko Ono (J.L. also sings backup on the record). It was Bowie's first time at **number ❶** in America, a position he danced back to eight years later with "Let's Dance." Music collectors may want to get their hands on "Little Drummer Boy," David's duet with the late Bing Crosby. It's as odd a pairing as rock 'n roll ever experienced - except, perhaps, when U2's Bono warbled with Frank Sinatra on ol' blue eyes' album, "Duets." Nothing odd about this bowie-tie pasta; it's a primo pasta dish destined to bring you a little *fame* when you serve it to dinner guests.

The Top 10 Ingredients

- ⅔ cup (or more) olive oil
- ½ cup fresh chopped basil
- 3 large garlic cloves, minced
- 2 medium Japanese eggplants, cut lengthwise into ½-inch slices
- 1 medium red onion, cut into ½-inch rounds
- 1 red bell pepper, quartered
- 1 yellow bell pepper, quartered
- 8 ounces bow-tie pasta
- 1 cup grated Parmesan cheese
- ⅓ cup toasted pine nuts

Serves 4

Blend ⅔ cup oil, chopped basil, and garlic in large shallow dish. Add eggplant slices, onion and bell peppers. Toss to coat. Season vegetables with salt and pepper. Cover and let stand 2 hours, which is enough time to catch David's weird movie, "The Man Who Fell To Earth."

Prepare barbecue and heat to medium. Drain excess marinade from vegetables and reserve. Grill vegetables until tender, about 5 minutes per side. Cool. Cut vegetables into ½-inch pieces.

Cook pasta in large pot of boiling salted water (plus 1 teaspoon olive oil) until tender, al dente. Drain. Transfer to large bowl. Add vegetables, reserved marinade, and ⅔ cup cheese; toss to combine. Season with salt and pepper. Add more oil if necessary to coat pasta. Sprinkle with toasted pine nuts and remaining Parmesan cheese. Serve and enjoy your 15 minutes of *fame*.

"Philadelphia Freedom" Cheesecake

Elton John

Follow the yellow brick road. Sounded like good advice to Reggie Dwight, your basic child prodigy studying at the Royal Academy of Music in London. Later, he teamed with lyricist Bernie Taupin, changed his name to Elton John and followed that road all the way to success. For three decades Elton has been a rock 'n roll superstar, with countless hit singles, including six at number ❶. Flamboyant, outrageous, quiet, pudgy, thin, gay, straight, druggie, clean...Elton's been there, done that. In 1994 he capped his recording career by copping an Oscar for his biggest hit to date, "Can You Feel The Love Tonight," from the animated feature, "The Lion King." "Philadelphia Freedom" is Elton's second biggest hit, a tribute to tennis star Billie Jean King. And now "Philadelphia Freedom" cheesecake is a tribute to that former student at the Royal Academy. It's rich and decorative - a lot like Elton!

The Top 14 Ingredients

Crust

18	vanilla wafer cookies
1	cup almonds, toasted
4½	tablespoons unsalted butter, melted

Filling

4	ounces imported white chocolate, chopped
2	8-ounce packages cream cheese
⅔	cup sugar
2	teaspoons vanilla extract
¾	teaspoon grated lemon peel
2	large eggs
¾	cup fresh raspberries

Topping

1	8-ounce container sour cream
3	tablespoons sugar
½	teaspoon vanilla extract
2	half-pint baskets raspberries
½	cup raspberry jam

Serves 12 (or 2 cheesecake lovers)

For Crust

Position rack in center of oven and preheat to 350°F. Butter 8x2-inch springform pan. Finely grind cookies and almonds in food processor. Add butter and blend until mixture forms moist crumbs. Using plastic wrap as aid, press crumbs firmly onto bottom and 2 inches up sides of pan. Bake until golden, about 10 minutes. Cool.

For Filling

Melt white chocolate in top of double boiler over simmering water until smooth, stirring often. Remove from over water. Using electric mixer, beat cream cheese, sugar, vanilla and peel in large bowl until smooth. Add eggs, beating just until combined. Beat in melted white chocolate.

Spoon half of batter into crust. Top with ¾ cup berries. Spoon remaining batter over. Bake until edges of cake are set but center is firm, about 45 minutes. Cool 20 minutes. Maintain oven temperature. Using fingertips, press down gently on edges of cheesecake to flatten sightly.

For Topping

Whisk sour cream, sugar and vanilla in bowl. Spoon over cake, spreading to edge of pan. Bake 5 minutes. Transfer cake in pan to rack. Run small knife around sides of cake. Cool completely. Chill cake overnight.

Lift cake pan off cheesecake. Transfer cheesecake to platter. Cover cake with berries. Bring jam to simmer in small saucepan, stirring often. Gently brush jam over berries. Is that gorgeous, or what!?

"Afternoon Delight"
Starland Vocal Band

A little nookie? A nooner perhaps? That was the inference in the song, "Afternoon Delight," which the Starland Vocal Band took to **number ❶** during the peak of the country's bicentennial celebration, July of '76. The 4 member band got a big career nudge from John Denver, who was still hot at the time, when he signed them to his newly formed record label, Windsong. "Afternoon Delight" was the only **number ❶** hit the record label ever had - a feat even Denver couldn't match. Even though the lyrics are considered sexually suggestive, "Afternoon Delight" was actually inspired from a menu (so claim the song's writers). Going full circle, the song now inspires this menu item, a superb stuffed artichoke. When served as a late afternoon appetizer, it's truly an *afternoon delight*. A roll in the hay will just have to wait until late afternoon when you've got something this delightful.

Serves 4-6

The Top 5 Ingredients

- 2 artichokes, trimmed
- ⅓ cup grated Parmesan cheese
- ⅓ cup Italian bread crumbs
- 1 teaspoon herbs de Provence
- olive oil

Using kitchen scissors, trim sharp points off tips of artichoke leaves. Place artichokes in vegetable steamer and steam until tender, about 30 minutes. Remove and let cool.

Preheat oven to 350°F. In small bowl, combine Parmesan cheese, bread crumbs and herbs de Provence. Open the artichokes, flower-like, and using a teaspoon, sprinkle cheese and bread crumb mixture down between the leaves. Place artichokes in a baking dish and dribble a little olive oil over the artichokes. Cover with aluminum foil and bake for 20 to 30 minutes. Serve hot or later at room temperature....or in bed, if you're really into *afternoon delight*.

"More Than A Filling"

Boston Pie

When it comes to cranking out albums quickly, no one can point a guilty finger at rock group Boston. Their first album was a speedy seven years in the making. Album two came a quick two years later, and their third zoomed in after an eight year hiatus. Boston's main man, Tom Scholz, claims he's a perfectionist. Tom, could you mean procrastinator!? Well, it doesn't take seven years to make "More Than A Filling" Boston Pie, but it isn't exactly a microwave quickie either. But is it good? Oh yeah...it's *more than a filling*!

Serves 8

The Top 11 Ingredients

Filling

- 2 cups milk
- 5 large egg yolks
- ¾ cup sugar
- 3 tablespoons flour
- 1 tablespoon Triple Sec
- 1 teaspoon vanilla extract

Cake

- 4 large eggs
- ⅔ cup plus 1 tablespoon sugar
- ¾ cup all purpose flour
- 2 tablespoons (¼ stick) unsalted butter, melted

Glaze

- ½ cup plus 2 tablespoons whipping cream
- 8 ounces semisweet chocolate, chopped
- 1 tablespoon Triple Sec
- 1 cup sliced almonds, toasted

For Filling

Scald milk in medium saucepan. Beat yolks, sugar and flour in medium bowl. Gradually whisk hot milk into yolk mixture. Return mixture to saucepan. Bring to boil and cook until thick, whisking constantly, about 3 minutes. Transfer to bowl. Stir in Triple Sec and vanilla. Cover with plastic wrap. Refrigerate until well chilled.

For Cake

Preheat oven to 375°F. Butter and flour 9-inch cake pan. Combine eggs and sugar in large bowl set over pan of barely simmering water. Using electric mixer, beat until just warm to touch. Remove from over water and beat until thick and tripled in volume, about 5 minutes. Fold in flour. Transfer ½ cup batter to small bowl; fold in butter. Gently but thoroughly fold butter mixture back into batter. Pour into prepared pan. Bake until toothpick inserted into center of cake comes out clean, about 18 minutes. Cool cake in pan 10 minutes. Turn out onto rack and cool completely. Cut cake into 2 layers. Place 1 layer cut side up on rack. Spread evenly with all of filling. Top with second cake layer cut side down.

For Glaze

Scald cream in small saucepan. Remove from heat and blend in chocolate. Stir until melted and smooth. Stir in Triple Sec. Let stand at room temperature until cool and thickened. Pour glaze over top and sides of cake. Press almond slices onto sides of cake. Refrigerate 1 hour.

"Dancing Queen" Sauce
on ABBA Swedish Meatballs

Bigger than Volvo? Who said rock 'n roll isn't big business? During the late '70s and early '80s, the Swedish group Abba was so successful they were a bigger export business for the scandinavian country than the mighty Volvo. In fact, the group was so popular worldwide they even outsold the Beatles. "Dancing Queen" was the group's only record to hit **number ❶** in America, which would have delighted any other group, but disappointed the Swedish quartet. They were used to topping the charts every time out in other countries around the world. Eventually, the disappointments, fights, and divorces among the foursome caused the group to break up in the mid-'80s, but chances are good they had put away a few corona for a rainy day. This recipe is a Swedish favorite, much the way Abba is fondly remembered. As anyone who saw the movie "Priscilla, Queen of the Desert" knows, Abba's fans were devoted to the point of raiding the bathroom for souvenirs.

The Top 9 Ingredients

1	pound ground veal
2/3	cup fresh white breadcrumbs
1/3	cup minced brown onion
1/4	cup minced red onion
1	large egg
3	tablespoons minced fresh dill
2	tablespoons vegetable oil
2/3	cup half and half
1/2	cup whipping cream

Serves 4

Line small baking pan with waxed paper. Combine veal, breadcrumbs, onions, egg and 2½ tablespoons dill in large bowl and blend well. Shape veal mixture into about 24 balls and place on prepared pan.

Heat oil in large skillet over medium heat. Add meatballs to skillet; cook until brown, turning frequently, about 12 minutes. Add half and half, whipping cream and ½ tablespoon dill to skillet; stir until sauce is slightly thickened, scraping up any browned bits, about 3 minutes. Season with salt and pepper and serve over cooked egg noodles. *Knowing me, knowing you…*we'll love it!

"Don't Stop" Eating

Fleetwood Mac-aroni and Cheese

Fleetwood Mac's "Don't Stop" has the distinction of being the first rock 'n roll Presidential theme song. Just as "Happy Days Are Here Again" will always be associated with FDR, "Don't Stop" now belongs to Bill and Hillary as well as Fleetwood Mac. The song is from the album "Rumors," which spent an amazing 31 weeks at the top of the album charts; second only to "Saturday Night Fever" as the biggest album of the '70s. Also from the album was the single, "Dreams," the group's only **number ❶** hit, although there were numerous others that charted in the Top 10. Now there's the delicious "Don't Stop" Fleetwood Mac-aroni and cheese. You'll find yourself reciting the song's lyrics when someone offers you a second helping of this creamy, dreamy dish. *Don't stop* - have some more!

The Top 17 Ingredients

- 1¾ cups elbow macaroni
- 3 teaspoons olive oil
- 2½ cups grated extra-sharp cheddar cheese (10 ounces)
- 1 cup sliced mushrooms
- 1 tablespoon dry Sherry
- 2 tablespoons plus 2 teaspoons all purpose flour
- 1½ teaspoons salt
- 1½ teaspoons dry mustard
- ¼ teaspoon ground black pepper
- ⅛ teaspoon cayenne pepper
- ½ teaspoon ground nutmeg
- 1⅓ cups half and half
- 1⅓ cups whipping cream
- ⅔ cup sour cream
- 2 large eggs
- 1 teaspoon Worcestershire sauce
- ⅓ cup grated Italian breadcrumbs

Serves 4

Preheat oven to 350°F. Lightly butter 13x9-inch glass baking dish. Cook macaroni in large pot of boiling salted water (plus 1 teaspoon olive oil) until tender, al dente, about 12 minutes. Drain macaroni. Transfer to prepared baking dish. Add half of the grated cheese. Meanwhile, add 2 teaspoons olive oil to medium skillet and sauté mushrooms over medium heat until tender. Add 1 tablespoon dry Sherry and continue to cook until Sherry evaporates.

Whisk flour, salt, mustard, black pepper, cayenne pepper and nutmeg in medium bowl. Gradually whisk in half and half, then whipping cream and sour cream. Add eggs, sautéed mushrooms and Worcestershire sauce; whisk to blend. Pour over macaroni in baking dish; stir to blend. Sprinkle remaining grated cheese over.

Bake Fleetwood Mac-aroni and cheese until edges start to brown, about 25 minutes. Remove from oven, reset oven to broil. Sprinkle breadcrumbs over the top of Fleetwood Mac-aroni and cheese and place under broiler until breadcrumbs brown, another 5 minutes. Remove and let stand 10 minutes before serving.

"Margaritaville" Pie

Jimmy Buffett

Jimmy Buffett - even his name suggests a smorgasbord, doesn't it?? The easy-going rocker had a big hit in '77 with "Margaritaville," which became his trademark song. When Jimmy isn't cruising the Caribbean (a favorite song subject) or drinking (a favorite among favorite song subjects) he even finds time to write his own cookbook. As a performer, he's been delighting his tequila guzzling fans for over 20 years. Think of "Margaritaville" Pie as a tequila cocktail gone bananas, literally. Do bananas and lime pie go together? Oh yeah! And after a few margaritas, they go even better!

The Top 14 Ingredients

Crust

- 1¾ cups all purpose flour
- ¾ teaspoon salt
- ⅓ cup chilled vegetable shortening, cut into pieces
- 5 tablespoons chilled unsalted butter, cut into pieces
- 7 tablespoons (about) ice water

Filling

- 10 large egg yolks
- 1 cup sugar
- ½ cup fresh lime juice
- ½ cup tequila
- 2 teaspoons grated lime peel
- ½ cup (1 stick) unsalted butter, cut into pieces

Topping

- 1 small very ripe banana, peeled
- 1 cup chilled whipping cream
- 1 tablespoon powdered sugar
- 1 lime for garnish

Serves 8

For Crust

Combine flour and salt in food processor. Add shortening and butter and cut in using on/off turns (or pulse) until mixture resembles coarse meal. Gradually blend in enough water until mixture forms moist clumps. Gather dough into ball; flatten into disk. Wrap in plastic wrap and chill 30 minutes. Meanwhile, enjoy a margarita!

Preheat oven to 350°F. Roll out dough on floured surface to 16-inch round. Transfer to 9-inch glass pie dish. Cut off excess dough, leaving ½-inch overhang. Fold overhang under to form double-thick edge. Crimp edge decoratively. Pierce crust with fork several times. Bake until crust is golden, piercing bottom if crust bubbles, about 35 minutes while you enjoy another margarita.

For Filling

Whisk first 5 ingredients in top of double boiler to blend. Set over simmering water and whisk until custard thickens and registers 170°F on a candy thermometer, about 4 minutes. Remove from over simmering water. Add butter and whisk until melted. Cool slightly. Pour filling into crust. Refrigerate until filling sets, at least 3 hours (or overnight) - time enough for a mitcher of pargaritas...I mean, pelcher of...pitcher of...oh, you know what I mean.

For Topping: Purée ripe banana in food processor. Using electric mixer, beat cream and sugar in medium bowl to stiff peaks. Fold banana into cream. Spoon topping over pie. Cut into wedges, garnish with lime slices, and serve...that is, if you can still (hiccup!) draw a sober breath.

"Rich Girls"

Hall and Oat Squares

Hall and Oates' musical career has had its share of ups and downs. After all, what do you expect for two people who met on an elevator? Trying to dodge a gang-fight on the streets of Philadelphia, Daryl and John both ducked into the same service elevator simultaneously, met, and have been singing the sounds of Philadelphia ever since. Their first few albums fared poorly, but they finally struck it rich with "Rich Girl." The single was their first **number ❶** hit, a position they'd return to 5 more times with songs like "Kiss On My List," "Maneater," and "I Can't Go For That." In fact, their string of hits ultimately made them the most successful recording duo in the history of rock 'n roll, according to Newsweek and Billboard magazines. So one could say "Rich Girls" was the start of making them rich boys. "Rich Girls" - Hall and Oat Squares aren't costly, but one bite and you'll understand just how rich they are. Serve them at holidays and no one will dare say, *"I Can't Go For That!"*

The Top 10 Ingredients

1½	cup all purpose flour
1½	cups old-fashioned oats
1½	cups firmly packed brown sugar
½	teaspoon baking soda
¼	teaspoon salt
¾	cup (1½ sticks) chilled unsalted butter, cut into pieces
1	12-ounce package semisweet chocolate chips
¾	cup unsalted peanuts
½	cup whipping cream
1	14-ounce bag caramels

Makes about 20 squares

Preheat oven to 350°F. Combine first 5 ingredients in food processor. Add butter and cut in using on/off turns until crumbs begin to stick together. Press all but 2 cups crumb mixture into bottom of 9x13-inch baking pan. Sprinkle chocolate chips and peanuts over. Set crust aside.

Bring cream to simmer in medium saucepan over medium heat. Add caramels and stir until melted and smooth. Pour caramel mixture over crust. Sprinkle reserved 2 cups crumb mixture over. Bake until edges are golden brown, about 15 minutes. Cut around pan sides to loosen. Cool completely. Cut into squares. Refrigerate squares until well chilled, about 3 hours. Serve cold. Even *Maneaters* will love these girls!

"Hotel California" Plate Special with "Heartache Tonight" Sauce

The Eagles

Check out time was near at "Hotel California." The Eagles were at their creative peak with the release of the "Hotel California" album - critics handed out accolades, colleagues handed out Grammys, and fans handed over cash to buy it. Yet no one realized it was the beginning of the end. The Eagles' next album, "The Long Run," which featured their final **number ❶** hit, "Heartache Tonight," was their final studio album. Had their fans known it would take fifteen years before the Eagles would reunite, "Heartache Tonight" would have taken on new meaning. "Heartache Tonight" Sauce will be popular and have a *long run* at your house, especially if served over "Hotel California" Plate Special, a colorful and tasty Cal-Mex dish. Not too much, though, or it'll be *heartburn* tonight!

The Top 11 Ingredients

"Hotel California" Plate Special

2	cups diced cooked chicken
1	medium onion, chopped
½	cup corn kernels
1	cup packed grated sharp cheddar cheese
¾	cup tomato sauce
1	4-ounce can chopped green chilies
2	large garlic cloves, minced
1½	teaspoons paprika
½	teaspoon cayenne pepper
1	cup Masa Harina (corn tortilla mix)
8	medium yellow bell peppers

Serves 8

For "Hotel California" Plate Special

In a bowl, combine all ingredients except Masa Harina and yellow bell peppers; stir. Add Masa Harina (corn tortilla mix) and stir until ingredients have thickened. Cut the tops off yellow bell peppers, remove seeds, and rinse. Stuff the peppers with the chicken mixture. Place them in a steamer with 1-inch of boiling water, cover. Steam until peppers are tender, about 30 minutes. Remove from steamer and top with "Heartache Tonight" sauce.

The Top 9 Ingredients

"Heartache Tonight" Sauce

- 5 dried New Mexico or California chilies
- ¼ cup olive oil
- 1 cup chopped onion
- 1½ teaspoons minced garlic
- 1 teaspoon ground cumin
- 1 teaspoon white pepper
- 1 tablespoon chopped fresh oregano
- 2 cups crushed tomatoes with purée
- ½ cup chicken broth

For "Heartache Tonight" Sauce

Cut chilies open and remove seeds. Boil chilies in a small pot of boiling water until soft, about 5 minutes. Drain chilies, reserving ¼ cup liquid. Purée chilies with reserved liquid in blender until smooth. Transfer chili paste to small bowl.

Heat olive oil in large skillet over medium heat. Add chopped onion and garlic and sauté until golden, about 7 minutes. Add ground cumin, white pepper, oregano, and chili paste. Cook another 2 minutes, stirring occasionally. Add tomatoes and broth. Reduce heat and simmer until thickened, about 40 minutes. Season to taste with salt and pepper. Place a tablespoon of sauce on the bottom of the plate, then add more to the top of each stuffed pepper. Garnish with sprig of cilantro.

"Running On Empty"

Jackson Brownies

From lean years to fat cats. During hard times in the '60s, Jackson Browne and his rock 'n roll roommates, J.D. Souther and Glenn Frey had to pool their meager resources to pay their $60/month rent. Browne found success first as a songwriter for Linda Ronstadt, Johnny Rivers, The Byrds, and Brewer & Shipley. Then in '72, he had a hit of his own with "Doctor My Eyes." Browne has been running full steam since then, giving concerts to save the environment and protest nuclear power, while still producing hits like "Running On Empty." Don't feel sorry for those roommates, either. They've done okay on their own. Now then, if you're looking for a healthy, delicious dessert that won't clog your arteries, try these "Running On Empty" Jackson (no cholesterol) Brownies. Your roommates will thank you for 'em.

The Top 9 Ingredients

1½	cups sugar
1	cup flour
¾	cup unsweetened cocoa powder
1	teaspoon baking powder
¼	teaspoon salt
¾	cup vegetable oil
4	egg whites, beaten
2	teaspoons vanilla extract
⅔	cup walnuts, chopped

Serves 6-10

Preheat oven to 350°F. Grease 8-inch square pan. Combine first 5 ingredients in large bowl. Add oil, egg whites, vanilla and blend. Stir in walnuts. Transfer to prepared pan. Bake until brownies are slightly puffed in center and edges are beginning to brown, about 30 minutes. Cover and chill overnight. Cut Jackson Brownies into squares...then rock 'n roll your teeth into 'em!

Chef Rex-ommendation! Jackson Brownies are better when served with "Blame It On The Sugar" - Milli Vanilla Ice Cream (see page 152) - even if the ice cream is loaded with cholesterol!

"You Don't Bring Me Flour"
Barbra Streisand & Neil Diamond

Remember the struggling songwriter for The Monkees? Well, that kid from Brooklyn did pretty good on his own, especially when he teamed up with another kid from Brooklyn, a funny girl named Barbra. The story goes...both Diamond and the other singing gem, Streisand, had recorded "You Don't Bring Me Flowers" independently, on separate albums, and had gone on with their lives. Then a Louisville disc jockey spliced the two cuts together, played it on the air, and fans went wild. Before long the Brooklyn kids were in the studio, nose-to-nose (no easy task!), recording the duet version. Afterwards, they bought "his-and-her" wheelbarrows to cart off their piles of money and Grammys. Now the tearjerking ballad has inspired "You Don't Bring Me Flour," a flourless cake, which will bring tears to your eyes - tears of joy, that is. Go ahead, have a second slice, but save some for your loved one, so they don't whine, *"You Don't Bring Me Flour Anymore..."*

Serves 10

Preheat oven to 350°F. Butter 9-inch springform pan with 2¾-inch-high sides. Line bottom of pan with parchment paper. Butter parchment. Combine 8 ounces chopped chocolate and butter in medium saucepan over low heat and stir until melted and smooth. Cool slightly.

Beat egg yolks and ½ cup sugar in large bowl until well blended. Stir in chocolate mixture. Using electric mixer, beat egg whites and 2 tablespoons sugar in large bowl until stiff. Using rubber spatula, gently fold beaten whites into chocolate mixture. Pour batter into prepared pan. Bake until puffed and toothpick inserted into center comes out with moist crumbs attached, about 30 minutes. Cool 10 minutes. Using small sharp knife, cut around sides of cake. Release pan sides. Invert cake onto rack. Peel off parchment and cool cake completely. Wrap in plastic wrap and refrigerate overnight while you listen to Barbra's and Neal's albums.

Beat chilled whipping cream with 3 tablespoons sugar and vanilla until soft peaks form. Transfer cake to platter. Cover top and sides with whipped cream. Press chocolate shavings and toasted almond slices onto sides of cake. Cover with cake dome and refrigerate.

The Top 8 Ingredients

- 8 ounces semisweet chocolate, finely chopped
- ½ cup (1 stick) unsalted butter
- 6 large eggs, separated
- ½ cup plus 5 tablespoons sugar
- 2 cups chilled whipping cream
- 1 teaspoon vanilla extract
- 4 ounces semisweet chocolate, shaved with vegetable peeler
- ⅓ cup toasted almond slices

"Night Fever" Pasta
with "Stayin' Aloaf"

The Bee Gees

Did you catch "disco fever"? It was the contagious result of big hits like the Bee Gees' "Night Fever" and "Stayin' Alive." The John Travolta movie, "Saturday Night Fever," was a box office smash and the Bee Gees' music from the film so dominated the charts, they rivaled the success achieved by Elvis and the Beatles. The "Saturday Night Fever" album sold over 25 million copies to become the best selling soundtrack of all time. The Bee Gees wrote and/or sang 9 of the Top 100 hits for the year (5 in the year's Top 10, including "Stayin' Alive" and "Night Fever"). And even after the soundtrack, the hits kept on coming. With songs like "Tragedy" and "Love You Inside Out," the Australian brothers hit **number ❶** 9 times during the late '70s. Once disco petered out and the dust had settled, Barry Gibb emerged as the second most successful songwriter of the rock era, right behind Lennon and McCartney. Barry and his brothers Gibb also wrote and produced other artists, including their younger brother, Andy, Barbra Streisand and Dionne Warwick. These recipes are very "Saturday Night Fever." It's a meal like the one John Travolta's family in the movie would have eaten...very tasty...very Italian. Dust off the old soundtrack and play it loudly as you prepare this delicious dinner. Catch the fever all over again!

The Top 12 Ingredients

"Night Fever" Pasta

- ¼ cup plus 1 teaspoon olive oil
- ¼ cup minced garlic
- 1 pound fresh linguine
- 1½ pounds skinless boneless chicken breasts, cut into thin strips
- 2 green chilies, seeded, cut into thinly sliced
- 3 plum tomatoes, seeded, diced
- ½ cup fresh chopped basil
- 4 ounces prosciutto, chopped
- 2 tablespoons (¼ stick) butter
- 1 cup grated Parmesan cheese
- ⅓ cup toasted pine nuts
  crushed red peppers

Serves 4

For "Night Fever" Pasta

Heat ¼ cup olive oil in large skillet over medium heat. Add garlic and sauté until brown, about 1 minute. Add chicken and sauté 5 minutes, stirring occasionally. Add green chilies and sauté another 2 minutes. Add tomatoes, ¼ cup basil, prosciutto and cook another minute or two. Remove from heat. Add butter and stir until melted.

Meanwhile, cook linguine in large pot of boiling salted water (with 1 teaspoon olive oil) until tender, al dente, about 3 minutes. Drain linguine and place in large pasta bowl. Add sauce and ½ cup Parmesan; toss to coat. Season with salt and pepper. Sprinkle with remaining basil, Parmesan, toasted pine nuts, and crushed red peppers.

The Top 8 Ingredients

"Stayin' Aloaf"

1   small loaf fresh Italian bread

4   ounces (½ package) soft cream cheese

¼   cup (½ stick) butter

¼   cup oil-packed sun dried tomatoes

1   tablespoon olive oil

1   teaspoon dried parsley flakes

½   teaspoon minced garlic

⅓   cup grated Parmesan cheese

For "Stayin' Aloaf"

Slice Italian bread in half, lengthwise.

In food processor, combine remaining ingredients (except Parmesan cheese) and blend, using pulse, until smooth. Spread mixture on each half of bread; sprinkle with Parmesan cheese.

Preheat broiler. Place bread halves under broiler until Parmesan starts to brown, about 3-5 minutes. Remove. Cut into slices and serve with "Night Fever" Pasta. Careful not to get any on your white polyester suit before you go out disco dancing!

"Hot Stuff" Salsa

Donna Summer

Hot Stuff pretty much describes Donna Summer's career in 1979. The reigning Disco Queen had the biggest hit of the year with "Hot Stuff," with yet another song, "Bad Girls," also in the year's Top 10. Donna went to **number ❶** again at the end of the year, this time teamed with Barbra Streisand on "No More Tears (Enough is enough)." That record became the battle of the divas, each trying to outwarble the other - and wearing out the listeners in the process. By the end of the song, anyone within earshot was

screaming, "Enough is enough!" That tiny complaint aside, Donna's big pipes and big hits have earned the *bad girl* a page in this rock' n roll recipe book. "Hot Stuff Salsa" is spicy, tasty, definitely hot, and great on a *summer's* eve.

The Top 10 Ingredients

¾	cup chopped fresh cilantro
3	cups diced tomatoes
¼	cup fresh red jalapeño chilies
1	green chili
1	small red onion
½	teaspoon minced garlic
¼	cup fresh lime juice
1	teaspoon salt
1	teaspoon ground black pepper
1	teaspoon ground cumin

Makes 4 cups

Coarsely chop each of first 6 ingredients separately in food processor. Place ingredients in medium bowl and stir. Add lime juice, salt, pepper, and cumin. Chill for 1 hour before serving with tortilla chips, potato chips or as a condiment. Don't be a *bad girl* and eat this *hot stuff* all by yourself. Share it with your disco-loving friends.

Chef Rex-ommendation!

Here's a hot idea for "Hot Stuff" Salsa. Add equal parts salsa and mayonnaise in bowl; stir. Add juice from a squeeze of lime; stir again. Use as salad dressing on tossed salad. Hot stuff!

"I Will Survive" Disco(unt) Dinner

Gloria Gaynor

"I Will Survive" was more than a **number ❶** smash for Gloria Gaynor, it was her anthem. For years the singer struggled to become the Queen of Discos, but Donna Summer was eventually crowned that title. Then, after spinal surgery, the death of her mother and other set-backs, Gloria gathered her remaining wits and had songwriters Perren and Fekaris pen "I Will Survive." The song became a disco classic because others, like Gloria, so identified with it. Therefore, this delicious dish is dedicated to all those trying to *survive*...on a tight budget. It's an economical meal that's easy on the pocket book, but tasty on the tongue.

The Top 10 Ingredients

6	fresh zucchinis
2	tablespoons olive oil
1	medium onion, chopped
8	ounces mushrooms, thinly sliced
1	green pepper, chopped
1	pound lean ground beef
1	small can tomato paste
1	can beef consommé
1	cup water
3	ounces dry french fried onion rings

Serves 6

Slice zucchinis in half, lengthwise. Place in large saucepan of parboiling water and blanch for 3 minutes. Remove from water; let cool. Scoop out the seeds and make "canoes" out of each zucchini. Reserve seed mixture.

In large skillet, heat 1 tablespoon olive oil and sauté onion, mushrooms, and green pepper until tender, about 8 minutes. Place in medium bowl and set aside. Add remaining olive oil to large skillet and sauté ground beef until brown and crunchy, scraping up bits from bottom of skillet occasionally. Add onion, mushroom, bell pepper mixture, tomato paste, consommé, water and zucchini seed reserve. Stir until well blended and cook over medium heat until liquid boils down by half and thickens, about 20-30 minutes.

Preheat oven to 350°F. In 13x9-inch glass baking dish, arrange zucchini "canoes" scooped side up. Spread the ground beef mixture from the skillet into each canoe and pour remaining mixture and sauce over the top, covering entire dish. Place onion rings on top and place in oven for 40 minutes. Remove from oven; let stand 10 minutes before serving.

"Y.M.C.A." (Yummy Mayonnaise, Crabmeat and Asparagus Salad)

The Village People

Working out at the Y.M.C.A. certainly paid off for The Village People. Those *macho men* scored the second biggest hit of 1979 with their tribute to the Young Men's Christian Association. The "village" referred to in their name is Greenwich and the "people" were six macho types sporting costumes that were popular with gays in the New York village at that time. Assembled by Casablanca record producer Jacques Morali, The Village People were the faves at discos and eventually got their own movie, "Can't Stop The Music," a movie so awful, it's actually fun to watch! Y.M.C.A. in this recipe stands for yummy mayonnaise, crabmeat and asparagus salad. And yummy it is. Oh, and don't worry, *men*...it's *macho*, too.

The Top 12 Ingredients

Dressing

1	cup mayonnaise
1	4-ounce can baby sweet peas, drained
1	tablespoon fresh lemon juice
1½	teaspoons tomato paste
1½	teaspoons minced shallots
½	teaspoon Dijon mustard
1	teaspoon fresh dill
¼	teaspoon pepper

Salad

1	pound asparagus, trimmed
8	ounces cooked crabmeat
4	large Boston or butter lettuce leaves
	fresh dill
	lemon wedges

Serves 4

For Dressing

Whisk first 8 ingredients in medium bowl to blend. Cover and refrigerate until ready to use.

For Salad

Steam asparagus on vegetable steamer in large pot with ½-inch boiling salted water until crisp-tender, about 4 minutes. Transfer to bowl of ice water and cool. Drain and pat dry. Mix crabmeat into dressing. Season to taste with salt and pepper. Arrange 1 lettuce leaf on each plate. Top with asparagus. Spoon crabmeat dressing over and serve. Garnish with fresh dill and lemon wedges.

"Reunited" Dessert

with Peaches and Herbs

Is success sweeter the second time around? Ask Herb. Even though Peaches and Herb were a fairly successful singing duo in the '60s, Herb quit to become a policeman in '70. He could arrest felons, but he couldn't arrest his desire to sing, so in the late '70s Herb teamed with a new Peaches. This time they achieved more success than before. "Reunited" spent 4 weeks at **number ❶** and placed in the Top 10 for the year. "Reunited," Dessert brings peaches and herbs together again. It's a sweet success that'll make you want to "*Shake your groove thing*" (their other big hit earlier that same year).

The Top 12 Ingredients

1	cup whipping cream
10	tablespoons sugar
¼	teaspoon vanilla
1	tablespoon fresh lemon juice
4	firm ripe peaches
¼	cup fresh mint, chopped
1½	cups flour
1½	teaspoons baking powder
½	teaspoon salt
¼	cup chilled vegetable shortening
3	tablespoons butter
½	cup milk

Serves 4

Beat whipping cream with 5 tablespoons sugar and vanilla until stiff peaks form. Cover and refrigerate.

Mix lemon juice with 1 tablespoon sugar in medium bowl. Peel and pit peaches. Slice thinly into bowl. Toss in lemon mixture. Set aside.

Preheat oven to 375°F. Place flour, baking powder, salt and remaining 4 tablespoons sugar into food processor and blend (using pulse). Add shortening and butter and blend (again using pulse) until mixtures resembles course meal. Gradually add ½ cup milk down chute and stir (again using pulse) until dry ingredients gather together, adding more milk if necessary.

Transfer dough to floured surface and knead 3 times. Divide into 4 equal pieces. Pat first piece of dough into patty-cake. Place on ungreased cookie sheet. Repeat with remaining dough. Bake until patty-cakes are light brown, about 22 minutes. Cool on sheet 5 minutes.

Place cakes into deep bowls. Spoon peaches and juices from bowl over each, dividing evenly. Top each with whipped cream, then sprinkle chopped mint leaves on top.

"What A Fool Believes"

The Doobie Broilers

Have you ever been a Doobie Brother? Anyone who has ever shared marijuana, a joint, or a doobie understands where the rockers' name came from. The group achieved its greatest success once singer/songwriter Michael McDonald joined the musical fraternity. He wrote the song, "What A Fool Believes," with rocker Kenny Loggins, intending it for Loggins' next album. However, the Doobies' producer, Ted Templeman, urged them to record it, too. Good thing, for it went to **number ❶** and earned the Doobies a truckload of Grammys. No wonder - it's a wonderful song - and the chicken dish its inspired is wonderful, too. Only *a fool believes* something this good is difficult to make. It's deceptively simple, yet so scrumptious. It may not win you any Grammys, but compliments will certainly be forthcoming.

The Top 9 Ingredients

- 1 ounce dried wild mushroom (porcini)
- 8 boneless skinless chicken breast halves
- ⅔ cup grated Parmesan cheese
- ¼ cup chopped fresh parsley
- 2 shallots, peeled
- 4 garlic cloves, minced
- 2 large eggs
- 4 tablespoons (½ stick) butter
  all purpose flour

Serves 6

Place mushrooms in small bowl. Pour over enough hot water to cover. Let stand until softened, about 30 minutes. Drain and chop mushrooms. Coarsely chop 2 chicken breasts. Place chopped meat, mushrooms, cheese, parsley, shallots, garlic, and eggs in food processor. Pulse until finely chopped. Season with salt and pepper.

Pound remaining breasts to ⅓-inch thickness. Divide filling among breasts, spreading onto each half breast. Fold over other half of breast to enclose filling. Secure with toothpicks.

Melt 2 tablespoons butter in each of 2 large skillets over medium heat. Season stuffed chicken breast with salt and pepper. Coat with flour, tap off excess. Add chicken to skillets; cook until brown, about 5 minutes per side. Cover and cook until chicken and stuffing are cooked through, about 6 minutes per side. Remove toothpicks and serve.

"Breakfast In America"
Supertramp Super French Toast

Breakfast in bed is what Supertramp could afford after the success they achieved with their album, "Breakfast in America." Founding members Rick Davies and Roger Hodgson first brought home the bacon with their '74 album, "Crime Of The Century," which sold one million - legally! But they were really cooking by the time they released their "breakfast" album in '79. Two cuts from the lp, "The Logical Song" and "Take The Long Way Home," placed in the Top 100 for the year. So it's only logical to include this super french toast recipe to the cookbook. It's a tasty twist on traditional french toast and a treat to serve at brunches, family gatherings, or after a late night rock concert. *Take the long way home* today by stopping off at the grocery store for the ingredients. You'll find that *breakfast in America* doesn't get any better than this.

The Top 10 Ingredients

- 2   tablespoons corn syrup
- ½   cup butter
- 1   cup firmly packed brown sugar
- 1   loaf french bread, crust trimmed
- 6   eggs
- 2   cups milk
- 1   teaspoon vanilla extract
- 1   teaspoon cinnamon
- ½   teaspoon ground nutmeg
- ¼   teaspoon salt

Serves 4-6

Combine the corn syrup, butter, and brown sugar in a small saucepan and simmer until syrupy. Pour this mixture over the bottom of a 9x13-inch casserole dish.

Slice the bread into 12 to 16 slices and place (crowd) the slices over the sugar-butter mixture in the dish.

In a bowl, beat together the eggs, milk, vanilla, cinnamon and nutmeg and salt and pour this mixture over the bread. Cover the dish and let it stand in the refrigerator overnight.

Preheat the oven to 350°F. Uncover the pan and bake for 45 minutes. Serve while hot. Super!

"The Piña Colada" Mousse

Rupert Holmes

"Escape (The Piña Colada Song)" didn't try to escape the **number ❶** position. The Rupert Holmes song lodged there for two weeks at the end of the decade and became a Top 10 song of the year. The clever lyrics told the story of a man, bored in his relationship, answering an ad in a singles' register, only to discover it's his girlfriend's ad. The song did wonders bringing estranged men and women together again - not to mention the wonders it did for the sale of Piña Coladas. Having written and produced songs for the likes of Barbra Streisand, Holmes went on to conquer other areas of show business, including Broadway. He adapted Dicken's novel and composed the music for "The Mystery of Edwin Drood," and took home the Tony award for Best Musical as a result. Serve this heavenly Piña Colada Mousse to your sweetheart and perhaps you'll rediscover one another. No matter what, for a dessert, it's a great *escape!*

The Top 9 Ingredients

1   cup canned cream of coconut
1   cup crushed pineapple
1½ cup whipping cream
¼   cup dark rum
2   tablespoons cold water
2   teaspoons unflavored gelatin
1   teaspoon vanilla extract
2   tablespoons sugar
    ground nutmeg

Serves 6

Purée cream of coconut, pineapple, 1 cup whipping cream and rum in blender. Transfer to bowl. Pour 2 tablespoons cold water in small sauce pan. Sprinkle with gelatin. Let stand 10 minutes. Stir over low heat until gelatin dissolves. Add gelatin mixture to coconut mixture; stir well. Divide mousse among 6 wineglasses or dessert dishes. Cover; chill for several hours or overnight. In separate bowl, whip remaining ½ cup whipping cream, vanilla, and sugar until soft peaks form. Top mousse with whipped cream and sprinkle with nutmeg.

Chef Rex-ommendation!

This dessert feels right at Holme when served with "Brown Sugar" - Rolling Stones Cookies (see page 91).

"Ooh Baby Baby" Back Ribs

Linda Ronstadt

Queen of the Remakes. That's the nickname Linda earned after remaking hits of others, such as the Everly Brothers' "When Will I Be Loved," Buddy Holly's "It's So Easy," and this song, Smokey Robinson and the Miracles' "Ooh Baby Baby." But Linda didn't just rest on the laurels of others, she's gone on to conquer more fields than any other contemporary singer. Rock 'n roll, pop standards, Mexican tunes, Gilbert & Sullivan - Linda's renditions wow critics and endear fans. Most of her records have been produced by Peter Asher, half the singing duo Peter & Gordon, popular during the early '60s. Now we pay tribute to Linda's lovely voice and her career risks by enjoying these baby back ribs. *It's so easy* to make them and *ooh baby baby* are they good.

The Top 12 Ingredients

- ½ cup vegetable oil
- 1 medium onion, chopped
- 12 garlic cloves, minced
- 4 cups "Careless Whimpers" Spicy Ketchup (see page 142)
- 2 cups beer
- 2 cups water
- 1 cup firmly packed brown sugar
- 3 tablespoons red wine vinegar
- 3 tablespoons dry mustard
- 4 teaspoons Worcestershire sauce
- 2 teaspoons Tabasco sauce
- 7 pounds pork baby back rib racks

Serves 4-6

Heat oil in large saucepan over medium-low heat. Add onion and sauté until soft, about 8 minutes. Add garlic and sauté 1 minute. Add "Careless Whimpers" Spicy Ketchup, beer, water, brown sugar, vinegar, mustard, Worcestershire and Tabasco sauce. Bring to boil, stirring occasionally. Reduce heat and simmer until reduced to 4 cups, stirring occasionally, about 1 hour 15 minutes. Cool.

Divide ribs between 2 large baking dishes. Brush with half of sauce. Cover ribs and remaining sauce separately and refrigerate overnight.

Prepare barbecue on medium-high heat. Grill ribs until tender, basting frequently with some of remaining sauce, about 30-45 minutes. Place remaining sauce in small saucepan and bring to simmer. Cut pork into individual ribs and place on platter. Serve immediately, with sauce on the side. Be sure to wash your hands before putting on another Linda Ronstadt CD - the sauce is messy!

Recipes of the '80s

"It's Still Rock and (Cinnamon) Rolls To Me"

Billy Joel

The amateur boxer from Hicksville, New York, decided not to take hits, but make hits. Hit records, that is. Billy Joel pulled no punches by establishing himself as a musical contender with the song, "Piano Man," which has also become his nickname. The piano man's albums sell in the millions, his concerts sell out, and animation cels bear his likeness and voice (Disney's "Oliver & Company"). In the mid-'80s, Joel married his *Uptown Girl*, model Christie Brinkley, but a decade and a daughter later the couple called it quits. Joel had his first **number ❶** hit in 1980 with "It's Still Rock and Roll To Me," the first of four **number ❶** hits. With the delicious "It's Still Rock and (Cinnamon) Rolls To Me" we now pay a chewy tribute to the rock 'n roll *piano man*, that former boxer from Hicksville, Billy Joel.

Makes about 15 rolls

Mix first 6 ingredients in large bowl. Add water, butter and egg and mix until smooth dough forms, about 4 minutes. Transfer dough to greased bowl. Cover with plastic wrap or clean towel. Let dough rise in warm draft-free area until doubled in volume, about 45 minutes. Take that opportunity to give another listen to the "52nd Street" album. It's still great rock 'n roll to me.

Butter 9x13-inch baking dish. Bring 1 cup brown sugar and ½ cup butter to boil in small saucepan. Boil 1 minute. Remove from heat and stir in ½ cup walnuts. Pour into prepared dish. Punch dough down. Roll out on lightly floured surface to 15x9-inch rectangle. Spread dough evenly with remaining ½ cup butter. Sprinkle with remaining ½ cup brown sugar and 1 tablespoon cinnamon. Sprinkle with remaining ½ cup walnuts and raisins. Roll up jelly roll style, starting at one long side. Slice dough into 1-inch-thick rounds.

Arrange dough slices cut side down in prepared dish, spacing evenly. Cover with plastic wrap. Let rise in warm draft-free area until doubled, again about 45 minutes. Why not check out "The River of Dreams" CD?

Preheat oven to 375°F. Bake rolls until lightly golden, about 20-25 minutes. Let stand 5 minutes. Turn out onto platter. Cool slightly. Serve warm.

The Top 14 Ingredients

- 1½ cups all purpose flour
- 1 cup whole wheat flour
- ¼ cup firmly packed brown sugar
- 1 envelope rapid-rise yeast
- ½ teaspoon salt
- ½ teaspoon ground cinnamon
- ¾ cup warm water
- ¼ cup (½ stick) butter, melted
- 1 egg
- 1½ cups firmly packed brown sugar
- 1 cup (2 sticks) butter
- 1 cup chopped walnuts
- 1 tablespoon ground cinnamon
- ½ cup raisins

"Another One Bites The Crust"

Queen

Queen reigned in 1980. "Another One Bites The Dust" was the **number ❶** song of the year and another Queen hit, "Crazy Little Thing Called Love," also placed in the Top 10 of that same year. Lead singer Freddie Mercury and fellow rockers were known for their theatrical and grandiose recordings, such as "Bohemian Rhapsody." That song charted in '75 and again in '92 when those far-out dudes, Wayne and Garth, made it popular all over again in the movie, "Wayne's World." It was a success Mercury didn't live to see ; he died of AIDS in the early '90s. This *crazy little pizza recipe called* "Another One Bites The Crust" is a delicious alternative to a traditional pizza smothered with red sauce, meat and cheese. Try it - you'll be crowned *Queen* for a day!

The Top 9 Ingredients

1½	ounces sun-dried tomatoes (about ½ cup)
¼	cup olive oil
2	large red onions, sliced
2	large red bell peppers, thinly sliced
2	1-pound Boboli crusts (baked cheese pizza crusts)
¾	cup olives
½	cup toasted pine nuts
½	pound soft goat cheese (Montrachet), crumbled
½	cup chopped fresh oregano

Makes 2 pizzas

Soak sun-dried tomatoes in ⅓ cup hot water; let soak for 20 minutes. Dice tomatoes.

Heat olive oil in large skillet over medium heat. Add sliced red onions and sliced red bell peppers and sauté until beginning to brown, stirring frequently, about 7 minutes.

Preheat oven to 450°F. Place Boboli on pizza pans or cookie sheets. Spread olives on each Boboli. Top each with half of onion mixture, sun-dried tomatoes, and pine nuts. Sprinkle with crumbled goat cheese. Bake until cheese softens, about 10 minutes. Remove from oven. Sprinkle with chopped fresh oregano. Cut pizzas into wedges and serve.

"Bette Davis Black Eye" Peas

Kim Carnes

Movie star Bette Davis never expected to be a rock 'n roll star, too. The song the movie legend's eyes inspired racked up statistics that would make anyone's eyes blink: it spent 9 weeks at **number ❶**, was the second biggest record of the year, the second biggest of the decade, went to **number ❶** in 21 countries and won Best Song and Record of the Year at the Grammys. Needless to say, it was a hard record for singer Kim Carnes to follow. Lucky for you, this recipe that the song and Bette's eyes inspired is easy to follow. Black eyed peas are a natural for a crockpot - the longer they cook, the better. Were she still alive today, Bette Davis would taste these black eyed peas, roll those famous eyes, and say, "I'd love to eat more, but I just washed my hair!"

The Top 12 Ingredients

1   tablespoon olive oil
1   small onion, chopped
1   shallot, minced
1   pound ground Italian sausage
1   16-ounce bag fresh black eyed peas (2 cups), rinsed, drained
1   cup chicken broth
1   small can tomato paste
1   bay leaf
1   tomato, seeded, chopped
    dash of Tabasco sauce

Serves 8

Heat olive oil in large skillet over medium-high heat. Sauté onion and shallot until tender, about 5 minutes. Add Italian sausage and cook until brown and flavorful.

Preheat oven to 250°F. Transfer sausage mixture to large baking dish. Add remaining ingredients and stir until well mixed. Salt and pepper to taste. Cover and bake in slow oven for 4-5 hours. Remove from oven; discard bay leaf. Let stand at room temperature for 5 minutes before serving.

Chef Rex-ommendation!

Serve this dish next New Year's Eve - black eyed peas are considered "good luck." But does it really work? Hey, the song went to **number ❶** in 21 countries, didn't it? Are you going to argue with that kind of success?

"Abracadabra" Sauce
Steve Miller Band

Rock 'n roller Steve Miller pulled a lucky rabbit out of his hat with "Abracadabra." The record was his third **number ❶** and the fourth biggest hit of '82. Steve started rockin' in the '60s and was really rollin' in the '70s with hits like "The Joker," "Rock 'N Me" and "Jet Airliner." Between hits and gigs, Miller retreats to his farm in Oregon, but every time he returns, he proves he still has that old rock 'n roll magic. In that vein, this recipe is a sauce that magically turns anything humdrum into something special. Serve it atop broiled fish and it's instantly a gourmet delight. Or warm the sauce in the microwave, serve it on a baked potato, and you'll discover the magic. *Abracadabra!*

The Top 6 Ingredients
4   large plum tomatoes
¼   cup chopped fresh basil
2   tablespoons chopped fresh marjoram
1   shallot, minced
2   tablespoons balsamic vinegar
1   tablespoon olive oil

Makes 2 cups

Bring medium saucepan of water to boil. Add tomatoes and blanch 1 minute. Drain. Transfer to medium bowl. Cover with cold water; cool. Peel tomatoes, cut in half; squeeze out juices. Chop tomatoes; transfer to bowl. Add herbs, shallot, vinegar, and 1 tablespoon olive oil; stir. Season with salt and pepper. Abracadabra, it's ready!

Chef Rex-ommendation!

Discover the sauce's magic when served on...

- "I Get A Round" Steak (see page 40)
- "Yellow Submarines" (see page 49)

"Down Under" Chicken
Men at Work

Those lads from 'down under' were certainly on top in '83. The Australian group, Men At Work, worked hard to place two songs at **number ❶** within three months of each other. The first was "Who Can It Be Now?" and the second, "Down Under," was so popular it even placed in the year's Top 10. On "Down Under," Colin Hay sang about the particular antics of Australian life, but judging by the enormous record sales worldwide, the song had universal appeal. "Down Under" Chicken is an Australian favorite and a complete meal, mate. You'll find its universal appeal, too, even if you live on the upper side of the equator. Now tie your kangaroos down, sport, and get to work making this great tasting "Down Under" Chicken.

Serves 4

For Sauce

Melt butter in medium saucepan over medium heat. Add onion and sauté, about 5 minutes. Add vinegar and peppercorns. Cook until almost no liquid remains in pan, about 3 minutes. Add both chicken and beef broths and simmer until reduced to ⅓ cup, about 20 minutes.

For Risotto

Preheat oven to 400°F. Melt butter in medium ovenproof saucepan over medium heat. Add onion and sauté, about 5 minutes. Add rice and cook 1 minute, stirring constantly. Add chicken broth, bring to boil. Cover, transfer to oven and bake until rice is tender and liquid is absorbed, about 15 minutes. Transfer to bowl and cool.

For Chicken

Prepare barbecue and heat to medium-high or preheat broiler. Pound chicken on both sides, then brush with oil. Season with salt and pepper. Grill chicken until cooked through, about 5 minutes per side.

Meanwhile, transfer rice to large saucepan. Mix in cream and cook over medium heat until heated through, stirring constantly. Mix in cheese. Season with salt and pepper. Cover and keep warm. Add tomatoes to sauce and simmer 4 minutes. Gradually whisk in butter. Season with salt and pepper. Cut chicken diagonally into slices. Arrange on plates. Spoon sauce over. Sprinkle with chives. Serve with risotto. Save any leftovers for your kangaroo.

The Top 12 Ingredients

Sauce

- 2 tablespoons (¼ stick) butter
- 1 small onion, chopped
- 3 tablespoons red wine vinegar
- 1 teaspoon crushed peppercorns
- 1 cup chicken broth
- 1 cup beef broth

Risotto

- 2 tablespoons (¼ stick) butter
- 1 small onion, chopped
- 1 cup rice
- 1¾ cups chicken broth

Chicken

- 4 boneless, skinless chicken breast halves
- vegetable oil

- ¼ cup whipping cream
- ⅓ cup grated Parmesan cheese
- 2 pounds tomatoes, peeled, chopped, drained
- 5 tablespoons butter, cut into pieces
- minced fresh chives

"Every Breath You Take" Garlic Chicken

The Police

The Police raided the top of the charts for 8 weeks in '83, and in the process, cuffed the **number ❶** hit of the year with "Every Breath You Take." The song was so popular it became the number four hit for the decade and even copped a Grammy for Record of the Year. Singer Sting and his fellow musicians, Andy Summers and Stewart Copeland, were at their peak of popularity during this period, but the big bust was near. By the mid-'80s, the Police decided to quit the force and pursue separate careers. Now then, should you find your refrigerator's been raided (either by police or family members) you'll be glad to know "Every Breath You Take" Garlic Chicken requires few ingredients, is simple to make, yet is absolutely delicious. However, after indulging in all that garlic, don't be surprised if someone standing near you sings that other Police hit, *"Don't Stand So Close To Me."*

The Top 7 Ingredients

⅓ olive oil

3 tablespoons herbs de Provence

2 tablespoons chopped garlic

1 4-pound chicken, cut in half

½ cup whole garlic cloves, peeled (about 16)

additional olive oil

fresh rosemary sprigs

Serves 2

Mix olive oil, herbs de Provence and garlic in small bowl. Add salt and pepper to taste. Place chicken cut side down on baking pan. Loosen chicken skin and rub garlic mixture under the skin of the breast and leg of each chicken half. Rub remainder of mixture on the outside of chicken. Cover, refrigerate overnight.

Preheat oven to 350°F. Toss whole garlic cloves with olive oil and place on and around chicken, along with fresh rosemary sprigs. Roast until chicken is almost cooked, about 45 minutes. Remove chicken from pan; reserve pan juices and garlic and discard rosemary.

Preheat broiler and broil chicken until cooked throughout, about 7 minutes. Place on serving platter, pour pan juices over top and serve.

"Beat It" Omelette

Michael Jackson

The 'gloved one' who gave us "Beat It" was hard to beat in '83. If there was a record to be broken in the rock 'n roll history books, Michael smashed 'em that year. First off, his album, "Thriller," became the biggest selling album of all time (over 40 million units and still selling), yielded 7 Top 10 hits and swept the Grammys. At year's end, the King of Pop had 3 hits in the Top 10 ("Billie Jean," "Say, Say, Say" and "Beat It") and 6 in the Top 100. In the years that followed Michael has proven himself to be a worldwide phenomenon, third only to the Beatles and Elvis Presley in chart accomplishments. Sure he's weird, his looks change, and his short marriage to Lisa Marie Presley had the world wondering what Neverland really meant...but, hey, nothing is *black and white* with Michael. In his honor, "Beat It" the omelette, is mostly vegetarian (depending on where you stand on the egg debate). It's tasty and when served with a dollop of sour cream - it becomes a *thriller!*

The Top 7 Ingredients

- 2 tablespoons (¼ stick) butter
- ½ cup chopped onion
- 6 eggs
- 2 green onions, sliced
- 2 ounces cream cheese, cut into small pieces
- ⅓ cup grated mozzarella cheese
- ⅓ cup grated Parmesan cheese

Serves 2

Preheat broiler. Melt 1 tablespoon butter in large ovenproof skillet over medium-high heat. Add onion and sauté about 5 minutes. Transfer onion to small bowl. Melt remaining 1 tablespoon butter in same skillet. Beat eggs in separate bowl (*beat it, beat it, beat it*) and add to skillet and season with salt and pepper. Cook until edges of omelet are set, about 1 minute. Lift edges of omelet and tilt skillet, allowing uncooked eggs to flow under cooked edges. Continue cooking until eggs are almost set, about 2 minutes. Sprinkle sautéed onion, green onions, cream cheese, and cheeses over omelet. Place in broiler until cheese melts. Remove from pan and cut omelet into wedges. Moonwalk over to the table and serve it.

"Sweet Dreams" (Are Made Of Cookies)

The Eurythmics

The Eurythmics, Annie Lennox and Dave Stewart, were as interesting to look at as they were to listen to. Over the years Annie has been a chanteuse chameleon (and usually an outrageous one) changing her looks from an orange butch haircut...to Mickey Mouse ears...to Renaissance attire. "Sweet Dreams" was the duo's only **number ❶** hit, among a slew of lesser hits, before the twosome became two onesomes, each pursuing separate musical careers. "Sweet Dreams" (Are Made Of Cookies) is sweet, dreamy, and like Annie's hair, very colorful.

The Top 13 Ingredients

Cookie Baskets

- ¼ cup sugar
- 3 tablespoons unsalted butter
- 2 tablespoons powdered sugar
- 1 teaspoon finely chopped aniseed
- ½ teaspoon vanilla extract
- ¼ teaspoon grated orange peel
- 3 tablespoons egg whites
- ¼ cup all purpose flour

Topping

"Blame It On The Sugar" - Milli Vanilla ice cream (see page 152)

- 1 pint basket strawberries, hulled, quartered
- 1 cup pineapple wedges
- 1 kiwi fruit, peeled, sliced

fresh mint leaves

Serves 6

For Cookie Baskets
Preheat oven to 325°F. Lightly butter and flour baking sheet. Whisk first 6 ingredients in medium bowl. Whisk in egg whites and flour.

Drop slightly rounded tablespoon of batter onto center of half of prepared baking sheet. Drop another slightly rounded tablespoon of batter onto center of second half of prepared baking sheet. Using back of spoon, spread each mound of batter to 6-inch round. Bake cookies until brown on edges, about 8 minutes. Working quickly and using metal spatula, lift 1 cookie off sheet. Immediately turn cookie over onto inverted custard cup. Gently flatten cookie on cup bottom; crimp sides of cookie. Repeat with second cookie. Remove cookies from cups. Rinse baking sheet under cold water; wipe sheet dry. Repeat process with remaining batter, first rinsing and drying, then buttering and flouring baking sheet between batches.

For Topping
Place cookie baskets on plates. Fill each with 2 small scoops of "Blame It On the Sugar" - Milli Vanilla ice cream. Top with fruit and mint leaves.

"Karmal Chameleonions"

on Culture Club Sandwiches

When it came to Boy George, rock critics didn't know whether to praise or ask for mascara tips. Credit George, the definitive gender-bender of the '80s, to sing original songs rather than remake obvious material like "Kind Of A Drag," or "Bette Davis Eyes." Boy George and his group, Culture Club, scored their biggest hit with "Karma Chameleon," a number ❶ smash in '84 that placed at number four in the year's Top 100. Whether you're a boy, girl, gay, straight, transvestite, cross-dresser...whatever, you'll enjoy these Culture Club sandwiches. The secret to making the onions sweet is to cook them slowly, on low heat. Mmm, and they are good, by George...er, *Boy George*.

Serves 4

Place 4 bread slices on work surface. Top with enough Parmesan cheese to cover bread evenly. Season with pepper. Top with 1 piece of ham and mozzarella cheese. Top each with another slice of bread. Add Canadian bacon and remaining Parmesan.

Heat large skillet over low heat. Add 1 tablespoon butter and sauté onion slowly, until caramelized, about 20 minutes. Add Sherry and stir until Sherry evaporates. Add onions to sandwiches and top with remaining bread slices, pressing sandwiches slightly.

Beat half and half and eggs together in large shallow dish. Add sandwiches and soak 3 minutes per side.

Add remaining butter to skillet and cook sandwiches until golden brown, about 4 minutes. Turn, cover pan and cook sandwiches until cheese begins to melt, about 6 minutes. Cool slightly. Cut sandwiches into quarters and serve.

The Top 10 Ingredients

12 slices egg bread
 4 ounces Parmesan cheese, grated
 4 ounces prosciutto ham slices
 4 ounces mozzarella cheese, grated
 4 slices Canadian bacon, cooked
 ⅔ cup half and half
 3 large eggs
 2 tablespoons butter
 1 large onion, sliced
 1 teaspoon dry Sherry

"What's Love Got to Do With It?"

Tuna Turner

What's friendship got to do with it? Well, ask good friends Annie Mae and Ann-Margaret. When Tina (nee: Annie Mae) left Ike Turner, she called her friend Ann-Margaret with whom she had co-starred in the rock movie, "Tommy." Annie Mae hid out at Ann-Margaret's for six months while Ike searched high and low for her. Once Tina finally dumped Ike, spiked her hair, and got her hands on this song, she scored with the biggest hit of her long career. "What's Love Got To Do With It" was **number ❶** for three weeks, was the second biggest hit of '84, and won Tina four major Grammys. A decade later, the song title also became a movie title as Tina's stormy marriage to Ike was brought to the silver screen. Tina has been charting since 1960 with songs like "Proud Mary" and, like the song says, she just keeps on rolling. We honor the dish Tina with this tuna dish. Love may not have a thing to do with it, but delicious flavor is the result when you put your heart into this recipe.

Serves 4

For Herb Paste
Finely chop all ingredients in food processor using on/off turns (or pulse). Season with salt and pepper. Let stand 3 hours at room temperature.

For Tuna Steaks
Prepare barbecue on medium-high heat. Spread 1 to 2 tablespoons Herb Paste over one side of each tuna steak. Place tuna on barbecue grill and cook 4 minutes, then turn. Spread top of each tuna steak with 1 to 2 tablespoons Herb Paste. Cook until tuna is cooked through, about 4 minutes more.

The Top 10 Ingredients

Herb Paste
- ½ cup lightly packed fresh cilantro leaves
- ½ large red onion
- ¼ cup olive oil
- 2 tablespoons fresh lemon juice
- 1 large garlic clove
- 1½ teaspoons ground cumin
- 1½ teaspoons turmeric
- 1½ teaspoons chili powder

Tuna Steaks
- 4 8-ounce (¾-inch thick) tuna steaks
  lemon wedges

"Caribbean Queen" Chicken Kebabs

Billy Ocean

The song was "European Queen" when released in Europe and was a great big...flop! Then the word "European" was dropped, "Caribbean" was inserted and the song was released in the US. *Suddenly,* (the name of the album, by the way) the song took off and hit **number ❶**. Billy has since returned to that position on two other occasions, with "There'll Be Sad Songs" and "Get Outta My Dreams, Get Into My Car," not to mention other songs that have placed in the Top 10. Not bad for a lad from Trinidad. "Caribbean Queen" Chicken Kebabs are a spicy island delight and especially good when served at a beach picnic near the ocean, be it the Pacific, Atlantic...or Billy.

The Top 15 Ingredients

- 8 garlic cloves, minced
- 2 teaspoons ground coriander
- 2 teaspoons ground turmeric
- 2 teaspoons dried mustard
- 2 teaspoons ground cloves
- 2 teaspoons chili powder
- 1 teaspoon aniseed
- 2 teaspoons parsley flakes

- 3 pounds boneless, skinless chicken breasts cut into 1-inch pieces
- 4 red onions, cut into 1-inch pieces
- 2 yellow bell peppers, cut into 1-inch pieces
- 4 zucchinis, cut into 1-inch rounds
- 1½ cups olive oil
- ⅓ fresh lime juice
- 12 bamboo skewers

Serves 6

Combine first 8 ingredients (spices) in small bowl. Place chicken in a glass baking dish and vegetables in another dish. Sprinkle half of spice mixture into each dish. Add half of olive oil and half of lime juice to each and coat well. Cover and refrigerate 6 hours.

Soak skewers in water 30 minutes. Drain. Alternate chicken and vegetables on skewers.

Prepare barbecue and heat to medium or preheat broiler. Season kebabs with salt and pepper. Grill until chicken is tender, about 5 minutes per side. Transfer to platter. *Get Outta My Dreams, Get Onto My Plate!*

"Raspberry Berets"

Prince

The artist formerly known as Prince was formerly known as Prince Rogers Nelson. Now known only by a symbol (oh, pleazzzze!), the former Prince from Minneapolis was dealt a royal flush when he released his "Purple Rain" soundtrack. "When Doves Fly" was the biggest hit single of '84 and "Raspberry Berets" was his fourth hit off the album. Over the years, the purple wonder has placed five tunes at number ❶, including, "Let's Go Crazy," "Kiss," "Batdance," and "Cream." His songs are often performed by other artists, such as Sinead O'Connor, who hit number ❶ with "Nothing Compares 2 U." "Raspberry Berets," the princely dessert, is a purple wonder, too. It's so good you'll want to jump in your *Little Red Corvette,* go back to the grocery store for more raspberries, and make it all over again.

The Top 9 Ingredients

Phyllo "Berets"

    nonstick vegetable oil spray

6 sheets phyllo pastry, thawed

¼ cup melted butter (½ stick)

Raspberry Soufflés

2 half-pint baskets raspberries

4 tablespoons plus ½ cup sugar

1 cup milk

½ cup (1 stick) butter, cut into pieces

½ cup all purpose flour

4 large egg yolks, beaten

6 large egg whites

Serves 6

For "Berets"

Preheat oven to 400°F. Arrange 6 small custard cups upside down on large baking sheet. Spray outsides of cups with vegetable oil spray. Lay 1 phyllo sheet on work surface; cover remaining phyllo with plastic and kitchen towel. Brush phyllo sheet lightly with melted butter. Lay another pastry sheet atop first sheet. Brush lightly with melted butter. Cut pastry stack into 4 equal-size squares. Lay 1 square stack, buttered side down, over 1 prepared cup, pressing gently to fit. Lay another square stack atop first square stack with corners at a different angle. Fold up any phyllo that is longer than cup and press to adhere to phyllo on custard cup. Brush outside of pastry with butter. Repeat with remaining pastry squares atop another custard cup. Repeat buttering, stacking, cutting and forming "berets" with remaining pastry sheets.

Bake phyllo until just golden brown, about 5 minutes. Transfer baking sheet to rack. Cool 10 minutes. Carefully remove pastry "berets" from custard cups. Arrange "berets" right side up on large baking sheet.

For Raspberry Soufflés

Purée berries in food processor until smooth. Strain into medium bowl to remove seeds. Stir in 3 tablespoons sugar.

Bring milk to a simmer in large saucepan. Remove from heat and stir in butter, flour and ½ cup sugar. Place saucepan over medium heat and stir until butter melts and mixture is thick, about 2 minutes. Remove from heat. Add egg yolks and whisk until smooth. Cool to room temperature.

Preheat oven to 400°F. Beat egg whites in large bowl until frothy. Add remaining 1 tablespoon sugar and beat until stiff peaks form. Stir ¾ cup raspberry purée into soufflé base. Gently fold beaten whites into soufflé base .

Divide soufflé mixture equally among phyllo pastry "berets." Bake until souffles are puffed and golden, about 20 minutes. Serve immediately.

"Careless Whimpers" Spicy Ketchup

served on Wham!burgers

Wham! That aptly describes the gangbuster success that Wham! had in '85. British heartthrobs George Michael and Andrew Ridgeley, collectively Wham!, had their first number ❶ hit with "Wake Me Up Before You Go-Go." They followed it with the biggest hit of the year, "Careless Whisper." They also hit the top of the charts one more time with "Everything She Wants" before George Michael decided - wham! - he wanted a solo career. On his own he's had 6 more number ❶ songs and in '87 once again had the biggest song of the year with his Grammy award winning, "Faith." Two of Michael's number ❶ hits have been duets with Aretha Franklin and Elton John. (Those two later teamed for a duet of their own, "Through The Storm." These artists love to play musical chairs, don't they?) "Careless Whimpers" Spicy Ketchup on Wham!burgers are hamburgers at their best. After tasting this special ketchup, you'll never want to go back to regular-old-boring-ketchup again. Put it on this spicy meat mixture and *Wham!* - you've got *everything she wants* - a great sandwich!

The Top 12 Ingredients

"Careless Whimpers" Spicy Ketchup

- 2 tablespoons olive oil
- ½ cup onion, minced
- ½ cup sliced green onions
- ½ cup red bell pepper, minced
- 3 jalapeño chilies, stemmed, minced
- 2 garlic cloves, minced
- 2 shallots, minced
- 1 teaspoon fresh chopped thyme
- 1½ cups bottled ketchup
- 1 large tomato, chopped
- ½ teaspoon white pepper
- 1 tablespoon brown sugar

Makes about 3 cups

For "Careless Whimpers" Spicy Ketchup

Heat oil in medium saucepan over low heat. Add all onions, bell pepper, chilies, garlic, shallots, and thyme. Cook until vegetables are tender, stirring occasionally, about 10 minutes. Mix in ketchup, tomato, white pepper, and brown sugar. Simmer until thickened, stirring occasionally, about 10 minutes. Cover and chill.

The Top 11 Ingredients

Wham!burgers

2⅔	pounds lean ground beef
1	tablespoon minced fresh thyme
1	tablespoon minced fresh parsley
1	teaspoon minced fresh rosemary
1	tablespoon Worcestershire sauce
⅓	cup Italian breadcrumbs
½	cup minced onion
1	egg, beaten
1	teaspoon seasoning salt
½	teaspoon pepper
8	hamburger buns (onion rolls, optional)

Serves 8

For Wham!burgers

Thoroughly combine all ingredients in medium bowl. Shape beef mixture into eight 1-inch-thick patties. Cover and chill at least 1 hour.

Prepare barbecue and heat to medium-high. Place burgers on grill. Cover grill and cook burgers 4 minutes. Turn burgers. Cover grill and cook burgers to desired doneness, about 4 minutes for medium-rare. Grill buns, cut side down, during last 2 minutes if desired. Serve Wham!burgers with "Careless Whimpers" Spicy Ketchup.

85

"Corn In The U.S.A."

Bruce Springsteen

The Boss had his way in 1985. "Born In The U.S.A." delivered more than 11 million sales, Springsteen's concert tour was the largest draw of the year, and his hit singles included "Dancing In The Dark" and the album's title cut. The New Jersey rocker rose to prominence in '75 with another "born" album, "Born To Run," and was one of the few individuals to ever make the covers of both Time and Newsweek the same week. Yet despite Springsteen's status as a rock 'n roll superstar, his Grammys, and even an Oscar for "Streets of Philadelphia," he's never had a number one hit single. His loyal blue collar fans don't hold it against him, though. Those same fans (and everyone else, too) will love this dish, "Corn In The U.S.A." Corn-on-the-cob gets roasted with this recipe and has never been better. Try it tonight if you've got a *Hungry Heart*, or better yet, a hungry tummy. It's *boss*.

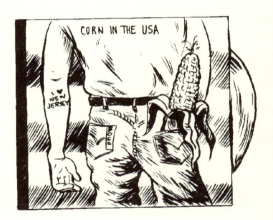

The Top 4 Ingredients

- 4 ears fresh corn on the cob with husks
- ½ cup butter (1 stick)
- 2 shallots, minced
- 4 tablespoons fresh chopped thyme

Serves 4

Soak corn in husks in cold water for 3-6 hours.

Prepare barbecue and heat to 3medium-high. Place corn in their husks on grill, turning occasionally. Grill until heated through, about 10-15 minutes. Husks will be charred.

Melt butter in saucepan over medium heat. Add shallots and thyme and sauté until translucent, about 4 minutes.

Remove husks from corn. Either spoon the shallot-thyme butter over corn and eat corn-on-the-cob style or remove corn from cobs and toss with shallot-thyme butter in medium bowl. Salt and pepper to taste.

"What Have You Cooked Well Done For Me Lately?"

Janet Jackson

Being a "Control" freak paid off for Janet Jackson - to the tune of $90 million! Janet was known primarily as Michael's little sister and child star of television sitcoms, "Good Times," and "Diff'rent Strokes." Her first two albums were flops, as was her marriage to James DeBarge of the singing DeBarge family. Then in '86, Janet teamed with record producers Jimmy Jim and Terry Lewis (formerly of the artist formerly known as Prince's group, Time) and the result was "Control." The album produced five Top 5 singles, and their next album together, "Rhythm Nation" had seven Top 5 singles, a record for any artist. Consequently, Ms. Jackson landed a $32 mil recording contract and her next one is worth $90 mil. She's a rock 'n roll superstar to rival her brother, Michael. "What Have You Done For Me Lately" was a big hit from her "Control" album and now the same question is asked of you. Why not cook "What Have You Cooked Well Done For Me Lately" and see if you don't get the respect you deserve. It's a terrific, hearty pork dish - a treat on a winter's eve. Make it tonight. Take *control!*

The Top 10 Ingredients

- 2 tablespoons vegetable oil
- 1¼ pounds pork tenderloins
- 2 tablespoons (¼ stick) unsalted butter
- 2 tablespoons chopped onion
- 2 tablespoons minced shallot
- ½ cup dry white wine
- 1 cup chicken broth
- ½ cup beef broth
- 1 cup whipping cream
- 2 tablespoons fresh lime juice

Serves 4

Preheat oven to 400°F. Heat oil in large ovenproof skillet over medium-high heat. Add pork and brown on all sides, turning frequently. Transfer skillet with pork to oven and roast pork until well done, about 20 minutes.

Meanwhile, melt butter in large skillet over medium heat. Add onion and shallot and sauté 5 minutes. Add wine and boil until liquid is reduced by half, stirring occasionally, about 5 minutes. Add both chicken and beef broths and boil until liquid is reduced to 6 tablespoons, stirring frequently, about 13 minutes. Add whipping cream and boil until sauce is reduced to 1 cup, stirring frequently, about 7 minutes. Mix in fresh lime juice. Season sauce to taste with salt and pepper.

Cut pork diagonally into ¼-inch thick slices. Spoon sauce onto plates. Fan pork atop sauce and serve.

"Addicted To Chocolate"

Robert Palmer

Music lovers became addicted to Robert Palmer's "Addicted To Love." The song was Palmer's first **number ❶** hit, thanks in part, to the popularity of the cloned "Palmer Girls" in his music video. Even Palmer became addicted - he used the sexy girls in following videos as well. The song takes a jab at people with addictive personalities, whether messed up on drugs, liquor, sex, or even love. Certainly chocolate falls into that category and "Addicted To Chocolate" Cake comes with a warning to all chocoholics out there: beware - major chocolate attack ahead! Serve it to fellow chocoholics and watch their eyes roll orgasmically to the back of their heads. You may find yourself singing another Palmer hit, *"I Didn't Mean To Turn You On!"*

The Top 11 Ingredients

Cake

- 1¾ cups water
- 1 tablespoon instant coffee powder
- 1 cup unsweetened cocoa powder
- 2¼ cup sifted cake flour
- 1½ teaspoons baking powder
- ¾ teaspoon baking soda
- ½ teaspoon salt
- 1 cup (2 sticks) butter
- 2 cups firmly packed dark brown sugar
- 2 large eggs
- 2 large egg yolks

Serves 12 (or 1 chocoholic)

For Cake

Preheat oven to 350°F. Lightly butter three (3) 9-inch cake pans. Line pan bottoms with waxed paper rounds. Butter the waxed paper.

Bring water and coffee powder to boil in small saucepan. Remove from heat. Add cocoa and whisk until smooth. Cool completely.

Sift flour, baking powder, baking soda, and salt into medium bowl. Using electric mixer, beat butter in large bowl until fluffy. Add sugar gradually, beating well and scraping down sides of bowl with rubber spatula occasionally. Add eggs and yolks, beating to blend. Mix dry ingredients and cocoa mixture into butter mixture. Divide batter evenly among prepared pans. Bake until toothpick inserted into centers comes out clean, about 20 minutes.

Cool cakes in pans on racks 10 minutes. Turn out onto racks. Peel off waxed paper; cool completely.

The Top 9 Ingredients

Frosting

1	teaspoon vanilla extract
1¼	cups whipping cream
½	cup sugar
4	large egg yolks
⅛	teaspoon salt
1	pound semisweet chocolate, finely chopped
¾	cup (1½) sticks butter
½	cup light corn syrup
¼	cup sour cream

For Frosting

In large saucepan, add vanilla, cream, sugar, yolks and salt and blend well. Stir over medium-low heat until custard thickens, about 7 minutes; do not boil. Mix in chocolate, butter and corn syrup. Remove from heat; stir until smooth. Mix in sour cream. Transfer frosting to bowl and refrigerate until spreadable, stirring occasionally, about 1 hour.

Place 1 cake layer on platter. Spread 1 cup frosting over. Repeat with second layer and frosting. Top with third cake layer. Spread remaining frosting over top and sides of cake, swirling decoratively. Sprinkle with white and milk chocolate shavings over top of cake. Serve immediately. Have another piece...then another...oh, just one more. *Addictive, isn't it?*

"I Still Haven't Found What I'm Cookin' For"

U2

What more could they possibly want? Success, fame, fortune, Grammys...and still U2 had the nerve to sing, "I Still Haven't Found What I'm Lookin' For." In 1987, the Irish rock group took that song to **number ❶**, as they did "With Or Without You," both from the Grammy winning Record of the Year, "Joshua Tree." Singer Bono and his emerald isle pals still find acceptance by selling out stadiums every concert tour, still find praise from rock critics, so perhaps what they've been looking for is this namesake recipe, "I Still Haven't Found What I'm Cookin' For." It's a side dish that's an Irish staple, and as popular as a four-sided shamrock. One taste and you, too...er, *U2* will agree.

The Top 7 Ingredients

4	pounds russet potatoes, peeled, cut into 1-inch pieces
1½	pounds cabbage, thinly sliced
1¼	cups water
1	cup milk
1	bunch green onions, chopped
¾	cup (1½ sticks) unsalted butter
	chopped fresh chives

Serves 6

Cook potatoes in large pot of boiling salted water until tender. Drain. Return potatoes to pot and mash with potato masher. Set aside.

Combine cabbage and water in large skillet. Boil until almost all liquid evaporates, tossing cabbage frequently, about 15 minutes. Mix cabbage into mashed potatoes.

Combine milk, chopped green onions and ½ cup butter in medium saucepan. Bring to boil, stirring to melt butter. Pour over potato mixture and stir. Season to taste with salt and pepper. Mound mashed potatoes in bowl. Make well in center. Place remaining ¼ cup butter in well. Sprinkle with chopped chives and serve *with or without you*.

"Knead You Tonight"

INXS Bread

Success was in excess for INXS in '88. The Australian band had paid their dues in the early '80s, producing 5 albums that were not exactly failures, but let's say, in excess of their demand. Then in 1988 they had the biggest hit record of the year with "Need You Tonight." The group's song and their tenacity have inspired this bread recipe - for slow and steady does it. Tonight you need to knead this bread. It has grains and seeds in excess, making it a hearty favorite, especially when served hot out of the oven. You'll find yourself wanting one slice after another, but try not to eat *INXS*.

Makes 1 loaf

Place cereal in large bowl. Pour 2 cups boiling water over. Let stand until mixture cools, about 20 minutes. Sprinkle yeast over cereal. Add 1 cup bread flour, oil, sugar, salt and stir until smooth. Gradually mix in enough remaining bread flour to form dough. Cover dough with plastic wrap; let rest 15 minutes in warm, draft-free area.

The Top 11 Ingredients

½	cup multi-grain cereal (7 grain)
2	cups boiling water
1	envelope dry yeast
4⅓	cups bread flour
1	tablespoon olive oil
1	tablespoon dark brown sugar
1½	teaspoons salt
2	teaspoons sesame seeds
2	teaspoons flax seeds
2	teaspoons poppy seeds
2	cups water

Turn out dough onto floured surface. Knead until smooth and elastic, adding more flour if sticky, about 10 minutes. Oil large bowl. Add dough to bowl; turn to coat. Cover bowl with plastic wrap. Let dough rise in warm, draft-free area until doubled, about 1 hour.

Mix all seeds in bowl. Punch down dough. Turn out onto lightly oiled surface. Knead briefly. Shape into 12x4-inch loaf. Sprinkle baking sheet with 2 teaspoons seeds. Place loaf atop seeds. Cover with plastic wrap. Let rise in warm, draft-free area until almost doubled, about 30-45 minutes.

Position 1 oven rack in center and 1 just below center in oven. Place baking pan on lower rack and preheat oven to 425°F. Brush loaf with water. Sprinkle with remaining seed mixture. Using sharp knife, cut 3 diagonal slashes onto surface of loaf. Place baking sheet with loaf in oven. Immediately pour 2 cups water into hot pan on lower rack in oven (water will steam).Bake loaf until golden and crusty and tester inserted into center comes out clean, about 35 minutes. Transfer to rack and cool.

"Rolls With It"

Steve Winwood & "Traffic" Jam

Roll with it - that philosophy sums up Steve Winwood's many musical reincarnations. Back in the '60s, at age 15, Steve joined The Spencer Davis Group. Despite their success, Winwood left to join his friends, Eric Clapton and Jack Bruce, in a group called Powerhouse. Their potency didn't last long, though, and Winwood next joined Traffic. After 3 albums, Traffic stalled, and Winwood again teamed with the ubiquitous Clapton and Ginger Baker to form Blind Faith. After that short-sighted stint, Winwood went solo and had finally achieved his biggest success in '86 with the Grammy award-winning number ❶ hit, "Higher Love." In '88, "Roll With It" was an even bigger hit and the third biggest hit of the year. That terrific song inspired these terrific rolls. And for once a *"Traffic jam"* is a pleasant experience. If you've never had tomato jam, well, you're in for a treat...*roll with it!*

The Top 14 Ingredients

Rolls

- ½ cup warm water
- 1 teaspoon active dry yeast
- 2 cups whole milk yogurt
- 2 cups all purpose flour
- 2 cups whole wheat flour
- 1½ cups rye flour
- 1 cup chopped walnuts, toasted
- 2 teaspoons salt

"Traffic" Jam

- 8 pounds ripe tomatoes, peeled, cored, puréed (3 quarts purée)
- 2 teaspoons salt
- 2 tablespoons sugar
- 4 tablespoons raspberry vinegar
- ½ teaspoon ground white pepper
- 4 tablespoons dark brown sugar
- 1 teaspoon ground cinnamon

Makes 16 rolls

For Rolls

Place warm water in large bowl. Sprinkle yeast over and stir to dissolve. Heat yogurt in small saucepan over medium-low heat until just warm to touch, stirring constantly. Add yogurt to yeast mixture. Gradually add all purpose flour and 1 cup whole wheat flour. Stir several minutes. Cover mixture with plastic. Let stand in warm draft-free area until springy and doubled in volume, about 1 hour.

Stir rye flour, toasted walnuts and salt into yeast mixture. Add enough remaining whole wheat flour to form dough. Knead on floured surface until smooth and elastic, adding more whole wheat flour if dough is sticky, 8 minutes.

Grease clean large bowl. Place dough in bowl, turning to coat completely. Cover with plastic. Let rise in warm draft-free area until doubled in volume and dough does not spring back when 2 fingers are gently pressed into side, about 2 hours.

Punch dough down. Let stand 10 minutes. Grease large cookie sheet. Divide dough into 16 equal pieces. Roll each piece into ball. Transfer to prepared cookie sheet, spacing evenly. Cover with plastic. Let rise in warm draft-free area until almost doubled in volume, about 40 minutes.

Preheat oven to 425°F. Bake until golden brown, about 35 minutes. Serve warm with butter and "Traffic" Jam.

For "Traffic" Jam

Makes 6 half-pint jars

Purée the tomatoes in batches in a food processor. Pour tomato purée into a large saucepan and place over medium heat. Stir in salt and sugar. Bring to full boil and continue to cook, uncovered for 1 hour; stirring occasionally. Mixture will be foamy, but will thicken and start to stick to bottom of the pan. At that point, add vinegar, pepper, brown sugar, and cinnamon and continue cooking until the jam is very thick, about 1 more hour.

Ladle jam into hot sterilized half-pint jars. Wipe rim of jars clean and seal jars with new lids and metal rings. Process in hot-water bath for 5 minutes.* Remove, cool, check seals, label and store. Allow to age for at least 2 weeks before using.

* Water bath procedure: place filled and sealed jars in boiling water, making sure that jar is completely submerged in boiling water. Boil for 5 minutes, remove from water, allow to cool.

"Blame It On The Sugar"

Milli Vanilla Ice Cream

Milli Vanilli or Phony Bologny? The duo, consisting of Rob Pilatus and Fabrice Morvan, had three **number ❶** hits, including "Blame It On The Rain." They even won a Grammy for Best New Artist before the world learned they were merely the most successful lip syncers in the music business. The fraud made headline news, their careers plummeted and the Grammy committee snatched back MV's trophy. (How times had changed! Twenty-five years before, no one seemed too upset that The Crystals didn't sing their **number ❶** hit, "He's A Rebel"). Now I know what you're wondering: is Milli Vanilla ice cream the real thing or some phony bologny recipe? You decide. Do some lip syncing of your own...or rather, let your lips sink into a bowl of this delicious, homemade ice cream today. Need more convincing? ...Didn't think so. If you put on a few pounds, just *blame it on the sugar.*

The Top 5 Ingredients

3	cups half and half
2	cups whipping cream
2	tablespoon vanilla
¾	cup sugar
9	large egg yolks

Makes about 8 cups

Bring first 3 ingredients to a simmer in saucepan over medium-low heat. Remove from heat, cover and let steep 40 minutes.

Return half and half mixture to simmer. Beat sugar and egg yolks to blend in medium bowl. Gradually whisk in hot half and half mixture. Return mixture to saucepan. Stir over medium heat until custard thickens, about 7 minutes; do not boil. Pour into large bowl. Refrigerate custard until well chilled.

Transfer custard to ice cream maker and process according to manufacturer's instructions. Freeze ice cream in covered container.

"Espresso Yourself"
Madonna

Like a virgin!? Well, perhaps only in the sense that it was Madonna's first time to have a number ❶ hit record. When the Material Girl first burst onto the music scene in '84, rock critics dismissed her as the "flavor of the day," granting her the 15 seconds of fame to which Andy Warhol claimed we're all entitled. Madonna not only proved them wrong, but as far as chart performance goes, has become one of the most successful females in the rock era, with eleven number ❶ songs. Singer, songwriter, music producer, actress, author, and occasional "flasher," Madonna does it all and does it outrageously. Sean Penn's former wife was among the first to use the music video to sell records in a big way. Many of her videos, like "Express Yourself," have outrageous budgets that could finance an entire movie for an independent film maker, like Sean. "Espresso Yourself" is an after dinner drink that's similar to Madonna Louise Veronica Ciccone in that it stands out in a crowd. Try it tonight for the first time and feel, uh...*like a virgin*!?

The Top 7 Ingredients

½ cup half and half
½ cup freshly brewed espresso coffee
2 tablespoons brandy
2 tablespoons white rum
2 tablespoons dark Crème de Cacao
   sugar
   semi-sweet chocolate shavings

Makes 2 servings

Whisk half and half in small saucepan over high heat until frothy, about 3 minutes. Divide espresso coffee between 2 cups. Add half of brandy, rum, and Crème de Cacao to each cup. Re-whisk half and half and pour into cups. Sweeten to taste with sugar and garnish with chocolate shavings. It's so good...*take a bow!*

Chef Rex-ommendation!

Here's a supreme suggestion - serve "Espresso Yourself" with "Where Did Our Love Biscotti" (see page 41).

"It Drives Me Crazy"

Fine Young Cannibal Salsa

Fine Young Cannibals drove "She Drives Me Crazy" all the way to **number ❶**. They also had a good thing going with their next **number ❶** hit, "Good Thing." Contrary to popular belief, this trio's name did not derive from their personal eating habits, but rather from the old Natalie Wood flick, "All The Fine Young Cannibals." This tasty salsa will drive you crazy, too, but don't worry - it contains no meat or carnage. What you decide to put the salsa on, however, is up to you. ...have you had a friend for lunch lately??

Makes about 2½ cups

Combine first 5 ingredients in medium bowl. Let stand 4 hours or overnight.

Prepare barbecue and heat to medium. Brush shiitake and oyster mushrooms on all sides with oil mixture. Reserve remaining oil mixture. Grill mushrooms until tender, turning occasionally, about 5 minutes. Cool. Coarsely chop mushrooms. Add grilled mushrooms, arugula, enoki mushrooms and red pepper to remaining oil mixture. Toss to combine.

The Top 10 Ingredients

¼ cup olive oil

1½ tablespoons balsamic vinegar

2 garlic cloves, minced

1 teaspoon black peppercorns, crushed

1 tablespoon chopped fresh thyme

6 ounces fresh shiitake mushrooms

6 ounces oyster mushrooms

¼ cup packed chopped arugula

1 3¼-ounce package enoki mushrooms, cut into thin lengths

¼ teaspoon dried crushed red pepper

Chef Rex-ommendation! This salsa will drive you crazy when served over squares of steamed polenta!

"Another Dish In Paradise"
Phil Collins

Who says you can't have it both ways? Most rock groups split up when members want solo careers, but not Phil Collins and Genesis. As a member of the rock group, Collins and friends have had great success, reaching **number ❶** in '86 with "Invisible Touch," along with many other Top10 singles. Yet on his own, Collins has done even better, with seven **number ❶** hits, including "Another Day In Paradise," the **number ❶** song of '89. And, as if both careers weren't enough, Collins even finds time for a movie career, starring in "Buster" and cameo roles in "Hook" and "A Hard Days Night." To salute all those careers, here's "Another Dish In Paradise." Asparagus, artichoke hearts and roasted peppers coming together in a cheese sauce and served on pasta is as close to *paradise* as we can get. It's so heavenly you'll want a second helping - so go ahead, *Phil* [sic] up your plate again.

The Top 10 Ingredients

- 3 large red bell peppers
- 1½ pounds rigatoni
- 1½ pounds asparagus, trimmed, cut into 1-inch pieces
- ½ cup artichoke hearts, cut into cubes
- 1 tablespoon olive oil
- ½ cup fine breadcrumbs
- 6½ tablespoons butter
- 6½ tablespoons flour
- 4½ cups milk
- 2¼ cups grated Fontina cheese
- 3 cups grated Parmesan cheese

Serves 4

Char peppers over gas flame or under broiler until blackened on all sides. Wrap in paper bag and let stand 10 minutes. Peel and seed peppers. Cut into ½-inch pieces. Using 2 tablespoons butter, grease bundt pan and coat with fine breadcrumbs. Bring large pot of salted water to boil. Add pasta and boil 12-15 minutes until pasta is tender, al dente. Transfer to large bowl. Steam asparagus until tender, about 5 minutes. Add asparagus and artichoke hearts to bowl. Add olive oil and toss mixture to coat.

Melt remaining butter in large saucepan over medium-high heat. Add flour and stir 2 minutes. Gradually add milk, whisking until smooth. Cook until sauce thickens, whisking frequently, about 8 minutes. Remove from heat. Add Fontina and Parmesan cheese and whisk until cheeses melt and sauce is smooth. Season with salt and pepper.

Preheat oven to 350°F. Add cheese sauce and peppers to pasta and vegetables and stir to coat. Transfer to prepared bundt pan. Cover with foil. Bake covered pasta until heated through, about 30 minutes. Loosen edges with knife and invert bundt pan onto platter. Garnish with fresh parsley sprigs.

Recipes of the '90s

"Nothing Compares 2 This Soup"
Sinead O'Connor

Are you angry? Bald?? Do you have this uncontrollable urge to rip up the Pope's picture on national television? Did you have a **number ❶** smash remaking Prince's "Nothing Compares 2 U"? If you answered "yes" to the first three questions - get therapy! If you answered "yes" to all four, guess what, you're Sinead O'Connor. What this angry, bald, Irish lass accomplishes musically, she lacks in public relations. Time and time again she lashes out at the public that she seeks. Maybe a cup of this delicious hot soup is what she needs to pacify her. Can't hurt. C 4 yourself. *Nothing compares 2 it!*

The Top 9 Ingredients

2 tablespoons olive oil

2 leeks, chopped

3 cups chicken broth

2 pounds celery root, peeled, cut into slices

1 pound russet potatoes, peeled, cubed

2 cups milk

¼ cup minced fresh parsley

3 tablespoons minced red onion

2 teaspoons grated orange peel

Serves 6

Heat oil in large saucepan over medium-low heat. Add leeks and sauté until tender, about 10 minutes. Add chicken broth, celery root and potatoes. Cover and simmer until vegetables are tender, about 45 minutes.

Purée broth mixture in batches in blender or processor until smooth. Return mixture to saucepan. Add enough milk to thicken soup to desired consistency. Season to taste with salt and pepper.

Combine parsley, onion, and orange peel in small bowl. Bring soup to simmer. Ladle into bowls. Sprinkle with parsley mixture and serve.

"Don't Cry"

Gunions N' Roses

Rock 'n roll trivia question: who was the famous rock 'n roll father-in-law to Guns N' Roses lead singer, Axl Rose? Rose and his buddies Izzy, Slash and others formed Guns N' Roses and became a big success for Geffen Records. In '88, they hit **number ❶** with "Sweet Child o' Mine" and another hit, "Don't Cry," was nothing to pout about in '91. The recipe named for that song will bring tears to your eyes - for you peel at least 16 onions to make the dish. Tears of joy will come later when you taste this creamy, oniony delight - a perfect side dish for holiday dinners. Now, to answer the question: who was Axl's father-in-law? Don Everly of The Everly Brothers. Unfortunately, Axl's marriage to Don's daughter Erin only lasted a month - it appears the bloom on the *Rose* faded fast.

The Top 10 Ingredients

- ¼ cup (½ stick) butter
- 6 leeks, sliced
- 2 large onions, sliced
- 8 shallots, halved
- 2 garlic cloves, minced
- 1 10-ounce bag frozen baby onions, thawed, drained
- 2 cups whipping cream
- 2 tablespoons dry breadcrumbs
- 2 tablespoons grated Parmesan cheese
- 2 tablespoons chopped fresh parsley

Serves 6

Melt butter in large skillet over medium heat. Add leeks, large onions, shallots and garlic and sauté until all are tender, about 20 minutes. Add baby onions and cook 10 minutes longer, stirring occasionally. Mix in 2 cups whipping cream. Boil until cream is thickened to sauce consistency, about 10 minutes. Transfer vegetable-cream mixture to a shallow baking dish.

Preheat oven to 425°F. Sprinkle breadcrumbs and Parmesan cheese over onion mixture. Bake until breadcrumbs and cheese are golden brown and onion mixture bubbles, about 20 minutes. Sprinkle with parsley. A rose on the table would be appropriate.

"Losing My Religion" Sinfully Good Pasta Sauce

R.E.M.

R.E.M. is a scientific term for rapid eye movement during sleep. Well, rapid eye movement is certainly what occurred as we watched "Losing My Religion" zoom up the music charts. The band R.E.M. hails from Athens, Georgia, and was considered an underground sound for 10 years before hitting it big time in '91. Their CD, "Out Of Time," was a timely success before their next monster hit named, appropriately, "Monster." Fans have accused rockers Michael Stipe and friends of 'selling out' by signing a $10 million record deal, but hey, who wouldn't!? "Losing My Religion" Sinfully Good Pasta Sauce is truly sinfully good and, in a confessional, I would have to admit - easy to make. It's enough to renew your faith in cooking, should you be losing yours.

The Top 9 Ingredients

15	ounces part-skim ricotta cheese
½	cup chopped fresh basil
½	cup sliced green onions (about 2)
½	cup roasted red bell pepper (available packed in jars), diced
¼	cup grated Parmesan cheese
¼	cup canned low-salt chicken broth
2	tablespoons olive oil
2	tablespoons dry white wine
2	garlic cloves, minced

Makes about 3 cups

This is a delicious and light summertime sauce. No cooking required.

Combine all ingredients in large bowl; stir to blend. Season to taste with salt and pepper. Easy enough?

Chef Rex-ommendation!

For a religious experience, serve on cooked pasta such as penne or fussili.

"Thyme, Love, and Tenderloins"

Michael Bolton

There's a lot of soul in the sound of soul provider Michael Bolton. For years he kicked around as a songwriter, supplying tunes for Air Supply, Barbra Streisand, Laura Branigan and The Pointer Sisters. But when Michael sang his own ballads - jackpot! His good looks, long locks, raspy vocals and romantic ballads have taken him to the top of the charts many times during the '90s. True, Michael takes his licks from rock critics and even when he won his Grammy, another winner earlier that evening made a snide remark about Michael's raspy voice by commenting, "...he sings with a hernia." Although Bolton's pride may suffer, his bank account swells, thanks to his faithful female fans. They loved his hit, "Time, Love and Tenderness," and now they'll love "Thyme, Love, and Tenderloins." It's the perfect date dinner. All you need (besides the ingredients) are wine, candlelight, and a Michael Bolton CD in the background doing the *soul providing*.

The Top 14 Ingredients

Herb Crust
- 2½ cups fresh breadcrumbs
- 2 cups chopped fresh parsley
- 3 tablespoons chopped fresh thyme
- ½ cup (1 stick) unsalted butter, melted

Sauce
- 1 bottle Cabernet Sauvignon wine
- ½ bottle tawny Port
- 2 cups canned beef broth

Beef and Potatoes
- 4 medium russet potatoes
- ¾ cup whipping cream
- 4 tablespoons olive oil
   ground nutmeg
- 4 1-inch thick beef tenderloin steaks
   paprika
- ¼ cup (½ stick) unsalted butter

Serves 4

For Herb Crust
Combine breadcrumbs with herbs. Pour butter over and mix well. Season with salt and pepper.

For Sauce
Pour red wine, Port and beef broth into large pot. Bring to simmer over medium-high heat. Continue to simmer until reduced to 1 cup, about 1 hour.

For Beef and Potatoes
Bring large saucepan of salted water to boil. Add potatoes and cook until tender. Drain potatoes and return to pan. Cook over low heat until dry, about 3 minutes. Peel warm potatoes; mash with potato masher. Using electric mixer, add cream and 2 tablespoons oil and beat until potatoes are smooth. Season with salt and nutmeg. Place potatoes in pastry bag fitted with ⅜-inch plain tip.

Season steaks with salt and pepper. Heat remaining 2 tablespoons oil in large skillet over high heat. Brown steaks about 4 minutes per side. Remove from heat and let stand 20 minutes.

Preheat broiler. Spread breadcrumb mixture on top of steaks, pressing to adhere. Broil until breadcrumbs are golden brown. Reduce oven to 450°F. Place steaks on ovenproof plates. Put potatoes onto plates and sprinkle with paprika. Transfer to oven and bake until potatoes and steaks are heated through, about 10 minutes. Heat sauce in medium saucepan. Whisk in butter until melted. Spoon sauce over steaks and serve.

"Give It Away"
Red Hot Chili Peppers Popcorn

Tube socks were never the same. Not after Red Hot Chili Peppers found a new way to wear them on their eye-opening album cover, "Abbey Road E.P." The socks covered only the band members genitals, shocking fans, parents, and especially tube sock wearers everywhere. When the Peppers dared to don only their socks at concerts, arrests for indecent exposure followed. It was a bit of a set back for the punk band whose reputation was red hot thanks to their CD, "Blood Sugar Sex Magik." The album produced the hit single "Give It Away," which is now a giveaway to this Red Hot Chili Pepper Popcorn recipe. It's a hot and spicy alternative to regular popcorn. So be adventurous - put on some tube socks (anywhere you want) and make a batch today. But don't keep it all to yourself...*give it away!*

The Top 4 Ingredients
¼ cup olive oil
5 dried red hot chili peppers
½ cup popping corn kernels
½ teaspoon chili powder

Makes 1 heaping bowl

Place chili peppers in olive oil and allow to marinate for several hours. Place 2 tablespoons oil marinade in saucepan and add popcorn. Cover and place over medium heat. Shake covered pan until popping stops. Remove from heat. Put popcorn in serving bowl and toss in with remaining oil marinade and chili powder. Time to *give it away*!

Chef Rex-ommendation! Spicy summertime snack when served with "Proud Marys" (see page 71).

"I Will Always Love Ewe" Stew

Whitney Houston

It took thirty-six years and Whitney's big pipes to dethrone the King. Elvis' record of having a song at **number ❶** for the longest time (11 weeks back in '56 for "Don't Be Cruel/Hound Dog") was shattered when Whitney sang Dolly Parton's song, "I Will Always Love You." The song held on for 14 amazing weeks, sending Elvis' hound dog to the has-been pound. The megahit was Whitney's 10th **number ❶** single in less than a decade, the **number ❶** hit of the year, and won every Grammy in sight. Well, what do you expect from Whitney - she comes from good stock: mother is Cissy Houston, backup singer extraordinaire, and cousin is the legendary singer Dionne Warwick. Hope there were no family spats in '86 when Dionne's **number ❶** hit, "That's What Friends Are For," was knocked out of the top spot by Whitney's "How Will I Know." Hey, Dionne, that's what relatives are for. "I Will Always Love Ewe" Stew is a lamb of a dish, I must admit sheepishly. The peanut butter and chilies make an interesting yet winning combination - kind of like Whitney and any song she sings.

The Top 13 Ingredients

- 2 tablespoons peanut oil
- 2 pounds lamb shoulder, trimmed, cut into 1-inch cubes
- 2 large onions, chopped
- 1 small can tomato paste
- 3 bay leaves
- ¼ teaspoon cayenne pepper
- 2 cups beef broth
- 2 cups water
- ¾ cup peanut butter
- 1 cup diced carrots
- 4 jalapeño chilies, seeded, diced
- 1 cup frozen peas
- cooked rice

Serves 6

Heat oil in large saucepan over medium-high heat. Add lamb and onions and cook until lamb is brown (which, by the way is Whitney's last name...married to singer Bobby Brown, but I digress...), stir occasionally, about 6 minutes. Mix in tomato paste, bay leaves and cayenne pepper and cook 1 minute. Season with salt and pepper. Add beef stock and water and bring to boil. Simmer until lamb is tender, about 1½ hours.

Stir peanut butter, carrots, and jalapeños into stew and cook until carrots are tender, about 30 minutes. Add peas and cook until heated through. Discard jalapeños. Serve stew over cooked rice. Get ready for your loved ones to declare, *"I Will Always Love You...if you promise to make this again!"*

"End of the Meal"
Boyznberry II Men(the) Parfaits

Girlz went crazy 4 Boyz II Men. At a time when most young black recording artists were cutting rap CDs (usually angry, to boot) along came the romantic ballads of Boyz II Men. This Motown group's fans found the Boyz' ballads the perfect antidote to rap music. No surprise then that Boyz' first CD, "Cooleyhighharmony," sold over 7 million copies and produced the huge hit single "End Of The Road." The song was the second biggest song of the year and was **number ❶** for a never-ending 13 weeks. It would have broken Elvis' record of 11 weeks ("Don't Be Cruel"/"Hound Dog") had Whitney Houston not just reset the record at 14 weeks with "I Will Always Love You." This dessert, Boyznberry II Men(the) Parfaits, is a delicious and romantic treat - just perfect for the *end of the road...*er, meal, uh...whatever.

The Top 11 Ingredients

Parfait

1	16-ounce bag frozen boysenberries, thawed
¼	cup sugar
1	tablespoon Crème de Menthe
½	teaspoon fresh lemon juice
¾	cup sugar
¼	cup water
6	large egg yolks
3	ounces white chocolate, melted
2	teaspoons vanilla extract
1⅔	cups chilled whipping cream

Sauce

1	16-ounce bag frozen boysenberries, thawed
¼	cup sugar
2	tablespoons Crème de Menthe

fresh boysenberries
fresh mint sprigs

Serves 6

For Parfait

Line 9x5-inch loaf pan with plastic wrap. Purée berries and ¼ cup sugar in blender until smooth. Strain. Measure 1⅓ cups purée and place in small saucepan. (Reserve any remaining purée for sauce.) Simmer purée over medium heat until reduced to 1 cup, stirring occasionally, about 8 minutes. Transfer to bowl and chill 30 minutes. Stir in Crème de Menthe and lemon juice. Refrigerate until ready to use.

Combine ¾ cup sugar, water, and yolks in medium metal bowl. Set bowl over saucepan of simmering water. Using hand-held electric mixer, beat yolk mixture until very hot, occasionally scraping down sides of bowl, about 8 minutes. Remove from over water. Add warm melted chocolate and vanilla extract and beat until cool. Beat whipping cream in another large bowl to stiff peaks. Gently fold whipping cream into chocolate mixture.

Transfer 1⅓ cups chocolate mixture to medium bowl. Fold in boysenberry purée. Fill prepared loaf pan (with the plastic wrap) with ⅓ of remaining chocolate mixture. Cover with berry-chocolate mixture. Top with remaining chocolate mixture. Smooth top. Freeze parfait overnight.

For Sauce
Purée frozen boysenberries, sugar and Crème de Menthe in blender or food processor until smooth. Strain. Add any berry purée reserved from parfait.

Unmold frozen parfait. Peel off plastic wrap. Slice into ½-inch-thick slices. Drizzle with sauce. Garnish with fresh berries and mint sprigs.

"Smells Like..." Nirvana Soup

Nirvana

Grunge music. It began in Seattle as an underground music movement - songs of anger, anguish, and angst. Nirvana played it and Generation X listened. Formed in '87, the group had its biggest success in '92 with the CD, "Nevermind," which shot to **number ❶** on the albums chart. "Smells Like Teen Spirit" from that CD smelled like a winner and remains their most successful song to date. Unfortunately, the angst and anger was not just a stage show, as lead singer and guitarist Kurt Cobain proved when he sought his nirvana by committing suicide in 1994. His act left behind a young daughter and wife, rocker Courtney Love (of Hole). And, coincidentally, like rockers Hendrix, Joplin & Morrison, Cobain was 27. If nirvana is about freeing the soul of the toxins of life, then this soup is a step in the right direction. It may not *smell like teen spirit* (whatever that smells like !?), but it certainly smells scrumptious.

Serves 8

Char bell peppers over gas flame or in broiler until blackened on all sides. Wrap pepper in paper bag and let stand 10 minutes to steam. Peel and seed. Keep yellow and red peppers separated.

Heat olive oil in large saucepan or pot over medium-high heat. Add onions, carrot, and celery and cook until tender, stirring occasionally, about 10 minutes. Add chicken broth, potatoes and bay leaf. Cover and simmer until potatoes are very tender, about 30 minutes.

Remove bay leaf. Pour half of soup into another large saucepan. Add yellow peppers to half of soup. Add red peppers to remaining half of soup. Purée yellow pepper mixture in blender or food processor in batches until smooth. Return to saucepan. Repeat with red pepper mixture, keeping soups separate.

Bring soups to simmer. Stir cilantro into yellow bell pepper soup and cumin into red bell pepper soup. Ladle both soups simultaneously into each bowl. Garnish with croutons and serve. Looks like heaven. Smells like...*nirvana*!

The Top 12 Ingredients

- 4 yellow bell peppers
- 3 red bell peppers
- 1 tablespoon olive oil
- 2 cups chopped onions
- 1 cup diced carrot
- ½ cup diced celery
- 6 cups chicken broth
- 2 russet potatoes, peeled, diced
- 1 bay leaf
- 1 tablespoon fresh cilantro
- ½ teaspoon ground cumin
   croutons

"Evenflow"

Pearl (Onion) Jam

Groucho Marx once stated, "I would never want to belong to a club that would have me as a member." Similarly, Pearl Jam's lead singer, Eddie Vedder, was quoted as saying he was depressed that so many fans relate to Pearl Jam's depressing music. The depressing truth is that Eddie Vedder and his fellow Pearl Jammers are mouthpieces for a generation of Americans raised by divorced parents and dysfunctional families. Like Nirvana, the heavy metal group also hails from the Seattle area and their album "Vs." sold nearly 1 million copies its first week of release. It set a record that even rock superstars like Michael Jackson have failed to match. For a recent concert tour, Pearl Jam teamed with rock veteran Neil Young, delighting two generations of rockers. Pearl Jam, the recipe, is a sweet yet unusual pearl onion dish. Try it as a vegetable side dish next Thanksgiving....or invite some depressed, grunge friends over and see if this delicious dish can't help cheer them up.

The Top 12 Ingredients

- 1 cup plus 1 teaspoon firmly packed golden brown sugar
- 1 cup water
- 2 cinnamon sticks
- 1 tablespoon chopped peeled fresh ginger
- 1 teaspoon grated lemon peel
- 1 10-ounce basket pearl onions
- 2½ tablespoons unsalted butter
- ⅛ teaspoon salt
- ¼ cup dried currants
- 3 tablespoons Madeira
- 1 teaspoon red wine vinegar
- 2 cups cranberries

Serves 6

Combine 1 cup sugar, water, cinnamon, ginger and lemon peel in medium saucepan over medium-high heat. Cook until sauce becomes syrupy, stirring occasionally, about 10 minutes. Set aside.

Blanch onions in medium pot of boiling water 4 minutes. Drain; rinse under cold water. Peel onions.

Melt butter in large skillet over medium-high heat. Add onions and sauté until beginning to brown, about 6 minutes. Mix in salt and remaining 1 teaspoon sugar. Add currants and stir 2 minutes. Add Madeira and vinegar and stir 1 minute longer. Add sugar mixture and 1 cup cranberries and cook 5 minutes, stirring often. Mix in 1 cup cranberries, cook until thickened, stirring often, about 5 minutes. Discard cinnamon sticks. Cover, chill for several hours in refrigerator. Let stand 30 minutes before serving.

"Disarm"ingly Good
Smashing Pumpkin Soup

Smashing Pumpkins - rock group or angry trick-or-treaters? Perhaps both as lead singer Billy Corgan describes the group as a "dysfunctional band." The group has suffered breakups, drug use, emotional turmoil...you know, your basic '90s stuff. Smashing Pumpkins' CD, "Siamese Dream," was a smashing success for the Chicago based band and produced the hit single "Disarm." To make the soup honoring the group, you needn't necessarily smash your pumpkin, but a good run through the food processor is a must. For skeptics who think pumpkin soup an oddity, try it. It'll become a favorite to serve at holidays and dinner parties. *"Disarm"*ingly good!

The Top 11 Ingredients

- 2 cups pumpkin, freshly processed
- 1 tablespoon olive oil
- 1 medium onion, sliced
- ½ chopped fresh parsley
- 1 clove garlic, minced
- ½ teaspoon grated nutmeg
- ½ teaspoon ground cloves
- 1 bay leaf
- 1 quart half and half
- 3 chicken bouillon cubes
- 6 teaspoons butter
   additional grated nutmeg

Serves 6

To process pumpkin: cut pumpkin into 8 sections; remove seeds. In large pot with boiling water, steam pumpkin until tender, about 45 minutes. Scoop out pumpkin from shell. Blend in food processor until smooth. Keep 2 cups for soup; freeze remainder in plastic ware for future use.

Heat olive oil in large saucepan on low heat. Add onion and sauté slowly until sweet and tender, about 10 minutes. Add parsley, garlic, nutmeg, ground cloves, bay leaf, and sauté 2 more minutes. Add half and half and heat until scalded. Add pumpkin, chicken bouillon cubes; salt and pepper to taste. Cook over low heat, about 15 minutes. Remove bay leaf. In blender or using hand blender, purée soup. Serve with a teaspoon of butter and grated nutmeg as garnish in each bowl.

"Nuttin' But A 'Pie' Thang"

Dr. Dre

D r. Dre certainly knows how to prescribe hit rap music. The rapper started his career with the group N.W.A. (if you don't know what the initials stand for - think Detective Mark Furhman). Hailing from Compton, south Los Angeles, Dr. Dre raps about drugs, violence, gangs, and street life. The graphic lyrics associated with rap music often shock and offend the establishment, but despite the critics' outrage, kids don't give it a bum rap - they listen. "Nuthin' But A 'G' Thang" was nuthin' but a big hit in '93, the 11th biggest of the year. This pie thang is sure to be nuthin' but a big hit around your house, too. Nuts and cranberries together - it's *nuthin' but "g"*...for good!

The Top 12 Ingredients

- 1   Pecan Allspice Crust (see page 55)
- ½   cup coarsely chopped walnuts
- ½   coarsely chopped pecans
- ½   cup sliced almonds
- ¾   cup firmly packed brown sugar
- ½   cup light corn syrup
- ¼   cup plus 2 tablespoons (¾ stick) unsalted butter, melted
- 3   large eggs
- 2   tablespoons light molasses
- 1   teaspoon vanilla extract
- ¼   teaspoon salt
- 1½ cups fresh cranberries, rinsed and drained

Serves 8

Preheat oven to 400°F. Combine walnuts, pecans, and almonds on cookie sheet. Toast nuts in oven until golden, about 5 minutes. Cool.

Whisk brown sugar, light corn syrup, butter, eggs, molasses, vanilla extract and salt to blend in bowl. Stir in toasted nuts and cranberries. Pour filling into prepared Pecan Allspice crust. Bake until center of filling is set, about 45 minutes. Cool pie completely.

"Let's Talk About..."
Salt-N-Pepa Seasoning Salt

Salt-N-Pepa spiced things up in rap music. The girls from Queens took on the predominantly black male arena of rap music and proved that females had something to rap about, too. Cheryl James and Sandy Denton met while working at Sears and decided rap, not retail, was their future. Later, they were joined by Spinderella (a.k.a. Dee Dee Roper) and together the trio has had hits like "Push It" and "Let's Talk About Sex." Instead, *let's talk about* this Salt-N-Pepa seasoning. It's a tasty, spicy alternative to the regular shaker stuffers. You may have to shop around to find these ingredients (and I don't mean Sears) but the extra mileage will be worth it.

The Top 2 Ingredients

9 tablespoons kosher rock salt

4 teaspoons Szechuan peppercorns or wild peppercorns (available in Asian markets and some specialty foods stores)

Makes approximately ⅓ cup

Combine salt and peppercorns in small skillet over low heat. Cook until aromatic and salt begins to turn color, stirring occasionally, about 10 minutes. Grind in mortar with pestle or in a spice grinder.

Chef Rex-ommendation!

Let's talk about how good this seasoning salt is on...

• stir-fry dishes

• "It's Too Late" Easy Potatoes (see page 89)

"I'd Do Anything For..."

Meat Loaf

Nicknames like Meat Loaf come easily when a kid in junior high weighs 240 pounds. So it was with singer, actor, Marvin Lee Aday. As an actor, (Meat Loaf portrayed Dr. Scott in the cult film, "Rocky Horror Picture Show") he auditioned for a New York musical written by Jim Steinman. That fateful meeting eventually led to the collaboration of Meat Loaf's 1977 album, "Bat Out Of Hell." That aptly describes how the album sold - as more than 25 million copies sold worldwide, making it one of the most successful albums ever produced. Despite the success, however, things went straight to hell. Steinman and Meat Loaf parted ways, they sued MCA for non-payment on royalties, and bankruptcy occurred. Then, after 8 years, Meat Loaf and Steinman reconciled, attempting a comeback with the CD, "Bat Out Of Hell II: Back In Hell." After so many years, odds were against success, but with the single, "I'd Do Anything For Love (But I Won't Do That)," fans proved they'd do anything for Meat Loaf. The song spent 5 weeks at **number ❶**, and placed in the Top 20 at year's end. To honor that comeback from hell, here's a meat loaf recipe worthy of Meat Loaf. Its delicious blend of meats, pistachios, and herbs will have your loved ones saying, *"I'd do anything for...a second helping."*

The Top 15 Ingredients

1	pound lean ground beef
½	pound ground pork
½	pound ground veal
2	cup chopped fresh spinach
1	cup Italian breadcrumbs
½	cup chopped pistachios
2	large garlic cloves, minced
1	teaspoon chopped fresh thyme
1	teaspoon chopped fresh rosemary
1	teaspoon ground nutmeg
2	large eggs, beaten
2	tablespoons Dijon mustard
	dash Tabasco sauce
	dash Worcestershire sauce
6	bacon slices

Serves 8 to 10

Combine beef, pork, veal, fresh spinach, breadcrumbs, chopped pistachios, garlic, thyme, rosemary, and ground nutmeg in bowl. Mix beaten eggs, Dijon mustard, Tabasco, and Worcestershire sauce into meat mixture and mix well. Season meat mixture with salt and pepper.

Preheat oven to 350°F. Line 9x5-inch glass loaf dish with bacon slices (used to flavor). Spread meat mixture into dish, rounding top. Cover and cook for 1½ hours.

OR...soak clay roaster in cold water for no less than 30 minutes. Remove from water. Place bacon slices on bottom of roaster. Spread meat mixture on top, round top. Put lid on roaster. Place in cold oven and heat to 450°F for 90 minutes.

Remove meat loaf from clay roaster or baking dish and discard bacon. Garnish with fresh rosemary sprigs.

"Dreamwhip Lover" Cake

Mariah Carey

Call her Hurricane Mariah. She was named after the song, "They Call The Wind Mariah," but the way this tiny girl with a BIG voice has stirred things up in the music biz, a hurricane reference is more appropriate. Read these many "firsts": Ms. Carey was the first artist ever to have her first five singles hit **number ❶**; the first to have her first 11 singles in a row make the Top 5. She's also the first female ever to debut a song in the **number ❶** position, which she did with "Fantasy" in '95. Her single, "Love Takes Time," took no time to become the biggest hit of the year 1990 (with another single, "Vision Of Love," also visible in the year's Top10). The **number ❶** hit, "Dreamlover," was a dream come true by being the third biggest hit of '93. So to Mariah's ability to make hit records appear quick and easy to make, we dedicate "Dreamwhip Lover" Cake. It's a yummy dessert that is quick and easy, yet can be decorated to become a *vision of love* when served at a party.

The Top 13 Ingredients

Cake
- 2¼ cups all purpose flour
- 1½ cups sugar
- 3½ teaspoons baking powder
- 1 teaspoon salt
- 1¼ cups milk
- ½ cup vegetable shortening
- 1 teaspoon vanilla extract
- 3 eggs

Filling
- 1 package Dream Whip
- 1½ cups cold milk
- 1 package (4 serving size) instant banana pudding
- 1 teaspoon vanilla extract
- 2 bananas, sliced
- 6 ounces semisweet chocolate, melted

Serves 12

For Cake
Preheat oven to 350°F. Grease and flour two (2) 9x2-inch round pans. In mixing bowl, beat all ingredients on low speed 30 seconds, scraping bowl occasionally. Beat on high speed 3 minutes, scraping bowl occasionally. Pour into prepared pans. Bake 30 minutes or until toothpick inserted in center comes out clean. Cool on wire rack; after ten minutes remove from pans and cool completely on wire rack.

For Filling
Beat Dream Whip and banana pudding in medium bowl with cold milk; add vanilla. Beat on HIGH until pudding mixture thickens and soft peaks form.

Place 1 layer of cake on cakeplate. Spread half the pudding mixture on cake (as if frosting). Place half of the banana slices on top of the pudding mixture. Place the other cake layer on top. Repeat process with pudding mixture and remaining banana slices. Drizzle melted chocolate decoratively over the entire cake. Refrigerate at least 2 hours before serving. Want some...*dreamlove*r?

"The Sign"
Ace of (Bouilla)Base

Ace of Base is a basic argument for siblings to get along. Jenny, Linn, and Jonas Berggren put their sibling rivalry aside, and along with their pal, Buddah, formed the quartet. Their pop, hip, fun, reggae sound made them one rich family - and the most successful Swedish rock group since Abba. "All That She Wants" was the second biggest hit of '93 and all that they wanted was for more success to follow. They got what they wanted, for the next year, their follow-up single, "The Sign," was the biggest hit of '94, with yet another single, "Don't Turn Around," also placing in the year's Top10. That kind of success has earned the Swedish rockers a rock 'n roll recipe. Granted, Ace of (Bouilla) Base isn't a Swedish recipe, but reggae isn't exactly Swedish either, so take it as *a sign* that anything goes. And should you hear someone nearby humming *"All That She Wants"* - chances are they mean another helping of this delicious bouillabase.

The Top 19 Ingredients

- 2 tablespoons olive oil
- 2 large onions, chopped
- 5 garlic cloves, minced
- 1 large leek, sliced
- 4 large tomatoes, coarsely chopped
- ½ cup chopped parsley
- 3 cups bottled clam juice
- 1 cup dry white wine
- 1 cup water
- 1 teaspoon grated orange peel
- ½ teaspoon cayenne pepper
- 1 tablespoon fresh chopped basil
- 1 tablespoon fresh chopped thyme
- 16 mussels
- 1 tablespoon salt
- 1 pound monkfish
- 1 pound scrod fillets
- 1 pound snapper fillets
- ½ pound bay scallops

Serves 8

In large pot, add olive oil and heat on medium-high heat. Add onions and garlic and cook until tender, about 5 minutes. Add leeks and cook until leeks are tender, about 10 minutes. Add tomatoes and reduce heat to simmer; cook for another 5 minutes. Add all remaining ingredients, except for the mussels, salt and fish. Cover and simmer for 30 minutes.

Wash the mussels under cold running water. Discard any that are open; soak the others for 30 minutes in a large pan covered with cold water (and 1 tablespoon salt). Drain them, scrub them, and put them in a saucepan with ½-inch water and cook over high heat, for 4 minutes, or until the shells open. Discard any mussels that do not open. Divide the mussels among 8 serving dishes.

To the simmering soup, add the monkfish, and simmer for 2 minutes. Then add the scrod, red snapper and simmer for 3 more minutes. Add the scallops, simmer for another 3 minutes. Ladle the soup and fish into the dishes containing the mussels. Garnish with chopped parsley.

"Linger"

The cranberries (sauce)

Perhaps the cranberries should have re-recorded Aretha Franklin's hit song, "Respect." Singer Dolores O'Riordan, her brothers Noel and Mike Hogan, and drummer Feargal Lawler were having trouble getting airplay in their native Ireland, so they decided to go abroad. When their CD, "Everybody Else Is Doing It, So Why Can't We?," sold 3 million copies and made them big names in the U.S., they finally got the respect they were looking for back home. Irish disc jockeys finally gave the public a taste of the cranberries. "Linger" was their big hit in '94, and linger is what the taste will do after you've sampled this yummy cranberry sauce. At holidays you'll never go back to familiar and traditional sauces after you've *lingered* on this one. Have a second serving - *everybody else is doing it, so why can't we?*

The Top 8 Ingredients

- 1 cup frozen cranberry juice concentrate, thawed
- ⅓ cup sugar
- 1 12-ounce package fresh cranberries, rinsed, drained
- ½ cup dried cranberries (2 ounces)
- 3 tablespoons orange marmalade
- 2 tablespoons orange juice concentrate
- 2 teaspoons minced orange peel
- ¼ teaspoon ground allspice

Serves 6

Combine cranberry juice concentrate and sugar in medium saucepan. Bring to boil over high heat, stirring until sugar dissolves. Add fresh and dried cranberries and cook until dried berries begin to soften and fresh berries begin to pop, stirring often, about 5 minutes. Remove from heat and stir in orange marmalade, orange juice concentrate, orange peel and allspice. Cool completely. Cover, chill until cold about 2 hours.

Chef Rex-ommendation!

As a substitute topping, let this sauce linger over "Philadelphia Freedom" Cheesecake (see page 104).

"Breathe Again" Sauce
on (riga)Toni Braxton

Y ou mean the world to me! That's what record producers Babyface and L.A. Reid probably said to Toni Braxton after her debut CD sold over 3 million copies. The CD produced two singles that placed in the Top 10 for the year '94, "Breathe Again," and, of course, "You Mean The World To Me." She even won a Grammy for Best New Artist. Not bad for a preacher man's daughter, who sang with her sisters in a group named, appropriately, "The Braxtons." But it was Toni as a solo who caught the attention of record producers Babyface and L.A. Reid. Together, with their savvy and her talent, these three had a year that would mean the world to anyone. "Breathe Again" Sauce on (riga)Toni is a terrific pasta dish made special by roasting the vegetables. The enhanced flavors will *mean the world to you* - and your loved ones.

The Top 13 Ingredients

4	large ripe tomatoes
2	medium white onions
1	whole garlic
1	large red bell pepper
3	whole ancho chilies
¼	cup corn oil
2	tablespoons sugar
1	cup water
1	teaspoon olive oil
1	pound rigatoni
½	cup half and half
8	ounces Ranchero cheese, crumbled
¼	cup fresh chopped cilantro

Serves 4

Prepare barbecue and heat to high. Roast tomatoes, onion, garlic, red bell pepper, and ancho chilies over open flame until charred, turning occasionally. Remove from grill. Allow to cool, then remove stems and seeds from chilies, red bell pepper, and tomatoes. Peel onion and garlic.

In medium saucepan, heat the corn oil on high until very hot. Add roasted tomatoes, onions, garlic, chili, red bell pepper, and sugar to saucepan. Cook for several minutes. Add water and simmer for about 30 minutes. Purée mixture in a blender or with hand blender. Salt and pepper to taste. Sauce should be slightly thick.

In a large pot, bring salted water (plus 1 teaspoon olive oil) to a boil and cook rigatoni until tender, al dente, about 12-15 minutes. Drain; place in pasta dish.

Add half and half to sauce and stir until heated. Pour sauce over rigatoni in a large pasta bowl. Top with crumbled Ranchero cheese and chopped cilantro. Serve immediately.

"Red Light Special" Spread

TLC

Don't assume that TLC stands for Tender Loving Care. It's short for T-Boz, Left Eye, and Chili. Still, this trio spent so much time on top of the charts in '95, Tender Loving Care must have had something to do with it. Their CD, "Crazysexycool," is the biggest selling CD for any female trio, surpassing records set by The Supremes and Wilson Phillips. It contained 2 **number ❶** hits, "Creep" and "Waterfalls," and another single, "Red Light Special," fell just short of **number ❶**. Record producers L.A. Reid and Babyface are again the duo behind the trio. With tender loving care, they produced the group's first CD, "Oooohhh...On The TLC Tip," which yielded 3 hits, including "Baby-Baby-Baby," the number 10 song of '92. This "Red Light Special" Spread is terrific on bread served with pasta dishes or fish entrees. It's guaranteed to impress your *crazysexycool* loved one with your culinary skills. And *baby, baby, baby*, is it good!

The Top 7 Ingredients

1	7-ounce jar roasted red bell peppers, drained
1	cup (8 ounces) cream cheese
1	tablespoon tomato paste
1½	teaspoons brown sugar
¼	teaspoon cayenne pepper
¼	teaspoon Tabasco
2	French bread baguettes, sliced

Serves 4

Purée red bell peppers in food processor. Add cream cheese, tomato paste, brown sugar, cayenne and Tabasco; blend. Season to taste with salt and pepper. Transfer to bowl.

Preheat broiler. Arrange bread slices on baking sheet. Broil until tops are golden brown. Turn bread slices over. Spread Red Light Special over slices. Broil until bubbling. Serve bread while hot...and with *TLC*.

Chef Rex-ommendation!

This "Red Light Special" is just as special when served on "Knead You Tonight" - INXS Bread (see page 149).

"Only Wanna Eat With You"
Hootie and the Grilled Fish

Expectations were shattered in '95, thanks to Hootie and the Blowfish. Expectations were...Michael Jackson's greatest hits compilation, "History," was supposed to make history by being the biggest CD of the year. But blowing away that competition was Hootie and the Blowfish. This soulful, doleful group from South Carolina rewrote Michael's "history" and never looked back by keeping their CD, "Cracked Rear View," on top of the album charts for a major chunk of the year. The Blowfish had a Top 10 hit with "Only Wanna Be With You," and now there's "Only Wanna Eat With You." It's grilled swordfish at its best. Of course, you can substitute blowfish for swordfish if you'd like. Frankly, I don't give a *hoot..ie*.

The Top 8 Ingredients

Salsa

1	cup Donna Summer's "Hot Stuff" Salsa (see page 118)
2	papayas, cubed
1	lime
⅓	cup chopped fresh cilantro

Swordfish Steaks

4	swordfish steaks
	olive oil
	fresh lime juice
	chili powder

Serves 4

For Salsa

Combine all ingredients in saucepan and cook over medium heat until just warm. Set aside.

For Swordfish Steaks

Place fish in a large shallow dish. Brush both sides with oil and lime juice. Sprinkle with chili powder.

Prepare barbecue and heat to medium-high. Grill fish until cooked through, about 4 minutes per side. Transfer to plates. Top with papaya salsa.

Chef Rex-ommendation! You'll only wanna eat this fish with "Garden Party" Salad (see page 95).

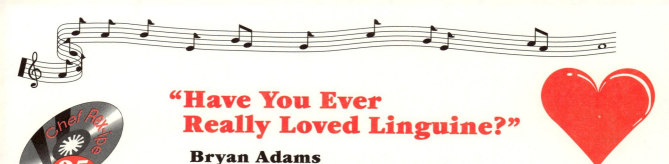

"Have You Ever Really Loved Linguine?"

Bryan Adams

His business card should read: "Have Movie Song, Will Record." Bryan Adams' first number ❶ hit was "Heaven," which hit the lofty spot two long years after he had recorded it for the movie, "A Night In Heaven." Then, in '91, he recorded "(Everything I Do) I Do It For You" for the movie, "Robin Hood, Prince of Thieves." Not only was it the biggest hit record of the year but it was nominated for an Oscar. In the U.K. the song was number ❶ for 16 weeks, the longest in British chart history. Next, the three musical musketeers, Bryan Adams/Sting/and Rod Stewart teamed up for "All For Love," for the movie, "The Three Musketeers." Most recently, the movie was the Marlon Brando, Johnny Depp film, "Don Juan De Marco," which contained the the number ❶ hit, "Have You Ever Really Loved A Woman." If Hollywood goes under, Bryan's career may be in jeopardy. So rent one of these movies tonight, make this recipe, and ask yourself, "Have You Ever Really Loved Linguine?" The answer will definitely be yes after you've tasted this rich, creamy, nutty pasta dish. It's surprisingly easy to prepare yet dinner guests will think you spent days in the kitchen prepping such a scrumptious dish. It's...*heaven*!

Serves 4

The Top 12 Ingredients

- 1 pound fresh linguine
- 1 pound Italian sausage (5 or 6 links)
- 1 red bell pepper
- 2 tablespoons olive oil
- 2 large shallots, chopped
- ½ teaspoon freshly ground nutmeg
- ¼ teaspoon cayenne pepper
- 1 cup chopped toasted walnuts
- ½ cup frozen peas
- ⅔ cup whipping cream
- ½ cup canned chicken broth
- ⅓ cup grated Parmesan cheese

Boil 2 quarts water in large pot. Cook fresh linguine until tender, al dente, approximately 3-5 minutes. Drain. Set aside.

Prepare barbecue and heat to medium-high. Grill sausages and red bell pepper, turning both after 5 minutes. Cook until sausages are done and red bell pepper is charred, about 8 minutes. Set sausages aside, and place pepper in a brown paper bag and allow to seep. After ten minutes, remove pepper from bag, remove seeds and dice.

Heat olive oil in large skillet over high heat. Add diced red bell pepper, chopped shallots, nutmeg, and cayenne and sauté about 4 minutes. Mix in ½ cup toasted walnuts and peas, stir, and continue to sauté 1 more minute. Cut grilled sausages into 1-inch thick slices and add them to the skillet. Then add cream and broth; boil until thickened to sauce consistency, about 6 minutes. Transfer linguine to pasta bowl. Add sauce and mix well. Top with remaining chopped toasted walnuts and sprinkle grated Parmesan cheese over all. Serve immediately.

Rock 'n Roll Party
Rex-ommendations

Make your next get-together a "Rock 'n Roll Recipe" party. These menu suggestions are all winners, but feel free to pick and choose other rock 'n roll recipes - after all, it's your party (and you can cry if you want to). Your guests will delight in the name of the recipes - not to mention rave at how tasty the dishes are. Having a rock 'n roll theme party is a terrific way to break the ice and start conversations when entertaining people who may not know one another. Strangers quickly turn into friends when rock 'n roll brings 'em together. Ask your guests to bring a favorite rock 'n roll album or compact disc. At Halloween, have your guests dress as a favorite rock 'n roller. Just have fun at your next rock 'n roll recipe party, be creative, play lots of golden oldies...and, hey, don't forget to invite me.

Little Rockers Birthday Party Menu

☆ Chicken "Lollypops"

☆ "Hang On Sloopys"

☆ "Classical Gas" Baked Beans

☆ "Mellow Yellow" Jellow

☆ "Johnny Angel"food Cake

"Hot Fun in the Summertime" Menu

☆ "Good Libations"

☆ "It's My Onion"
(And I'll Cry If I Want To)

☆ Wham!burgers with "Careless Whimpers" Spicy Ketchup

☆ "Corn in the U.S.A."

☆ "You Ain't Seen Nothin' Yet" Slaw

☆ "Strawberry Pie Forever"

"That's What Friends Are For"
Fun Times/Fun Food Menu

☆ "Great Balls Of Fire"

☆ "Light My Fire" Salad

☆ "Breath Again" Sauce - on (riga)Toni Braxton

☆ "Knead You Tonight" INXS Bread
   with "Red Light Special" Spread

☆ "Philadelphia Freedom" Cheesecake

"I Got You, Babe"
Romantic Dinner For Two Menu

☆ "An Hors (d'oeuvre) With No Name"

☆ "Smells Like..." - Nirvana Soup

☆ "Love Me Tender"loin

☆ "Evenflow" - Pearl (Onion) Jam

☆ "Espresso Yourself"

☆ "Where Did Our Love Biscotti?"

Rockin' Holiday Dinner

☆ "One Of These Delights"

☆ "Disarm"ingly Good -
   Smashing Pumpkin Soup

☆ Roasted Turkey

☆ "Gouda Golly Miss Molly" Potatoes

☆ "Don't Cry" - Gunions & Roses

☆ "Linger" - the cranberries (sauce)

☆ "Rolls With It"

☆ "American Pie"

A Bunch For Brunch Menu

☆ "Proud Marys"

☆ "Afternoon Delight"

☆ "Wake Up Little Susies" with Buddy Holly-daise Sauce

☆ "Woodstock" Favorite -
   Crosby, Stills, Hash & Young Chicken

☆ "Tossin' 'n Turnin' " Salad with "Sherry" Vinaigrette

☆ "How Can You Mend A Broken Tart?"

Conversion Charts

Liquid & Dry Measure Conversions

Metric amounts shown (deciliters, liters, grams, kilograms) are the nearest equivalents.

a pinch	=	slightly less than ¼ teaspoon				
a dash	=	a few drops				
3 teaspoons	=	1 tablespoon				
2 tablespoons	=	1 ounce	=	¼ deciliter (liquid), 30 grams (dry)		
1 jigger	=	3 tablespoons =		1½ ounces		
8 tablespoons	=	½ cup	=	4 ounces	=	1 deciliter
16 tablespoons	=	1 cup	=	½ pint	=	¼ quart
2 cups	=	1 pint	=	½ quart	=	1 pound* = ½ liter (liquid), 450 grams (dry)
4 cups	=	32 ounces	=	2 pints	=	1 quart = 1 liter
16 cups	=	4 quarts	=	1 gallon	=	3¾ liters
8 quarts (dry)	=	1 peck	=	7¼ kilograms		
4 pecks (dry)	=	1 bushel				

* Dry ingredients measured in cups will vary in weight.

Butter, Shortening, Cheese and Other Solids

1 tablespoon	=	⅛ stick	=	½ ounce	=	15 grams
2 tablespoons	=	¼ stick	=	1 ounce	=	30 grams
4 tablespoons	=	½ stick	=	¼ cup	=	2 ounces = 60 grams
8 tablespoons	=	1 stick	=	½ cup	=	4 ounces = 115 grams
16 tablespoons	=	2 sticks	=	1 cup	=	8 ounces = 225 grams
32 tablespoons	=	4 sticks	=	2 cups	=	16 ounces = 450 grams

Flour (unsifted)

1 tablespoon	=	¼ ounce	=	8.75 grams
¼ cup	=	1¼ ounces	=	35 grams
⅓ cup	=	1½ ounces	=	45 grams
½ cup	=	2½ ounces	=	70 grams
⅔ cup	=	3¼ ounces	=	90 grams
¾ cup	=	3½ ounces	=	105 grams
1 cup	=	5 ounces	=	140 grams
1½ cups	=	7½ ounces	=	210 grams
2 cups	=	10 ounces	=	280 grams
3½ cups	=	16 ounces	=	490 grams
		(1 pound)		

Note: 1 cup sifted flour = 1 cup unsifted flour minus 1½ tablespoons.

Granulated Sugar

1 teaspoon	=	⅙ ounce	=	5 grams
1 tablespoon	=	½ ounce	=	15 grams
¼ cup (4 tablespoons)	=	1¾ ounces	=	60 grams
⅓ cup (5 tablespoons)	=	2¼ ounces	=	75 grams
½ cup	=	3½ ounces	=	100 grams
⅔ cup	=	4½ ounces	=	130 grams
¾ cup	=	5 ounces	=	150 grams
1 cup	=	6¾ ounces	=	200 grams
1½ cups	=	9½ ounces	=	300 grams
2 cups	=	13½ ounces	=	400 grams

Recipe Index

Artist Index

Books Available from InfoPlus

Safer Sex - Guidelines to Live By

Are you one of the million people infected with HIV, the virus that causes AIDS, and doesn't even know it? This complete and up-to-date reference book about safer sex tells you what's safe, what's not. The easy to read book also contains information about sexually transmitted diseases, HIV testing, condoms, lubricants and spermicides. Order your copy today!

Rock 'n Roll Recipes

Over 150 fun and easy recipes inspired by classic rock 'n roll songs and artists. Chef Rex Havick has cooked up a cookbook, rock trivia book, and rolled 'em into one! A great gift! Order more copies now!

Order Form

Book	Quantity	Price Each U.S./Canada	Total
Safer Sex - Guidelines to Live By		$4.95/$6.50	
Rock 'n Roll Recipes		$16.95/$21.95	
		SubTotal:	
	Sales Tax (Add 8.25% for books shipped to California addresses):		
		Shipping:	
		Total:	

Shipping

Book rate - $2.00 for the first book, 75 cents for each additional book.
(Surface shipping may take three to four weeks.)
Priority Mail - $3.00 per book.

Payment - Payable in U.S. Funds only. No cash orders accepted.

❏ Check or Money Order: Payable to InfoPlus.

Credit Card: ❏ VISA   ❏ MasterCard

Card Number: _____   Expiration Date: _____

Name on Card: _____

Signature: _____

Or for Credit Card orders, call or fax this form to 818-403-0416

Name: _____

Company: _____

Address: _____

_____

City: _____   State/Zip: _____

Send to: InfoPlus
1012 Fair Oaks Avenue, Suite 124
South Pasadena, CA 91030